WORLD HISTORY ATLAS

Contents

©2005 Maps.com, 120 Cremona Drive, Santa Barbara, CA 93117 / 800-929-4MAP / 805-685-3100. Second printing with revisions.

Cover image: World map by Frederick deWit, 1660. Image from digital collection by Visual Language Library.

Visit the world's premier map website at http://www.maps.com for thousands of map resources, including driving directions, address finding, and downloadable maps. For additional educational map collections and resources, visit http://www.maps101.com.

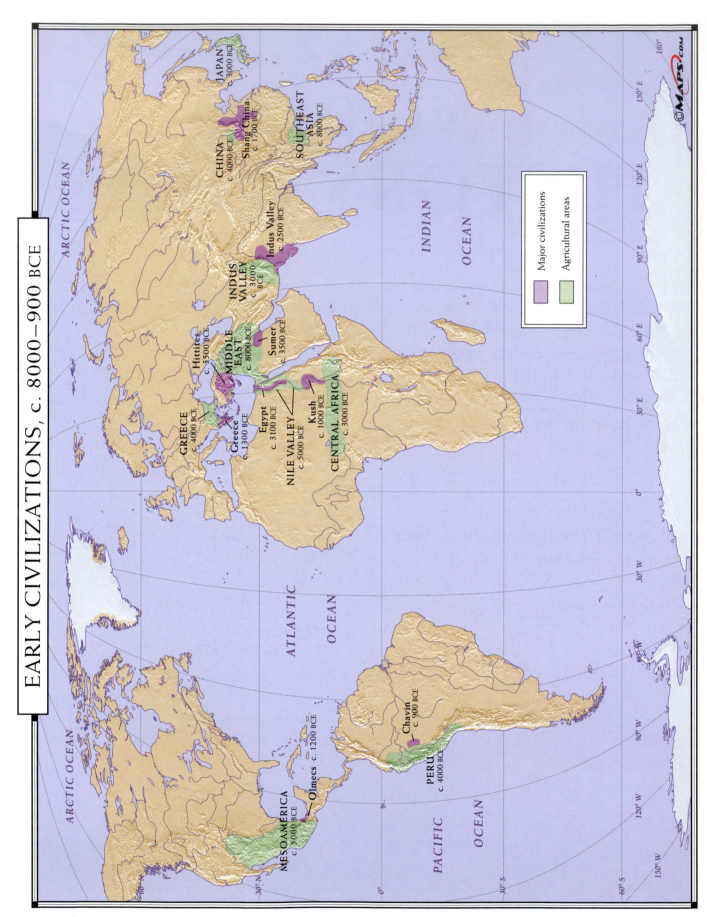

EARLY CIVILIZATIONS, c. 8000–900 BCE

ARCTIC OCEAN

JAPAN c. 3000 BCE

CHINA c. 4000 BCE

Shang China c. 1700 BCE

SOUTHEAST ASIA c. 8000 BCE

Indus Valley c. 2500 BCE

INDUS VALLEY c. 3000 BCE

MIDDLE EAST c. 8000 BCE

Hittites c. 3500 BCE

Sumer c. 3500 BCE

GREECE c. 4000 BCE

Greece c. 1300 BCE

Egypt c. 3100 BCE

NILE VALLEY c. 5000 BCE

Kush c. 1000 BCE

CENTRAL AFRICA c. 3000 BCE

INDIAN OCEAN

Major civilizations

Agricultural areas

ATLANTIC OCEAN

PACIFIC OCEAN

Chavin c. 900 BCE

PERU c. 4000 BCE

MESOAMERICA c. 5000 BCE

Olmecs c. 1200 BCE

©MAPS.com

THE SPREAD OF AGRICULTURE, c. 10,000–1000 BCE

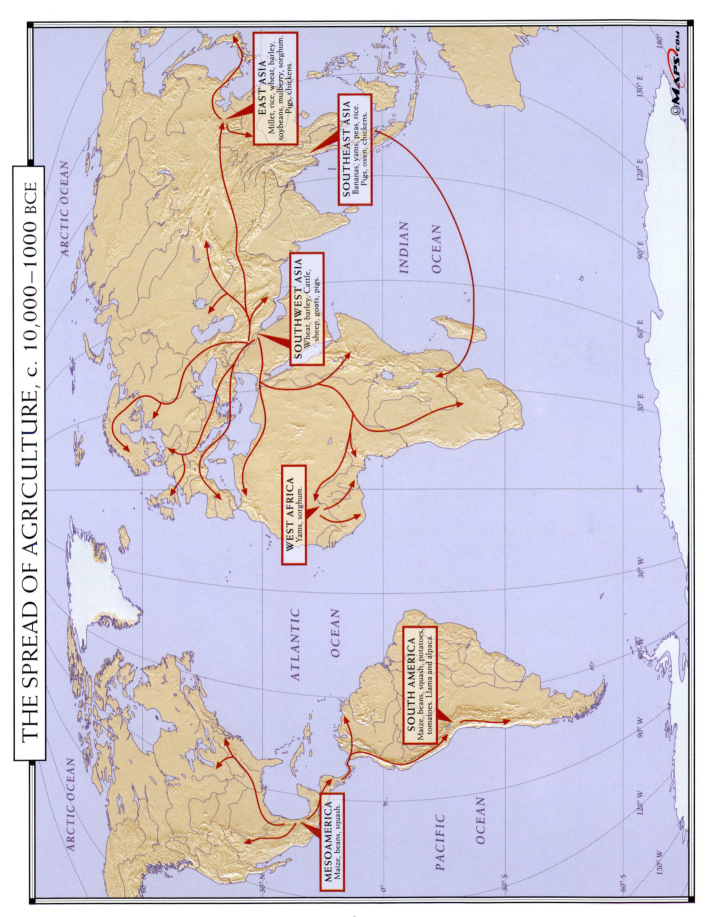

EAST ASIA
Millet, rice, wheat, barley, soybeans, mulberry, sorghum. Pigs, chickens.

SOUTHEAST ASIA
Bananas; yams, peas, rice. Pigs, oxen, chickens.

SOUTHWEST ASIA
Wheat, barley. Cattle, sheep, goats, pigs.

WEST AFRICA
Yams, sorghum.

SOUTH AMERICA
Maize, beans, squash, potatoes, tomatoes. Llama and alpaca.

MESOAMERICA
Maize, beans, squash.

ARCTIC OCEAN

INDIAN OCEAN

ATLANTIC OCEAN

PACIFIC OCEAN

©MAPS.com

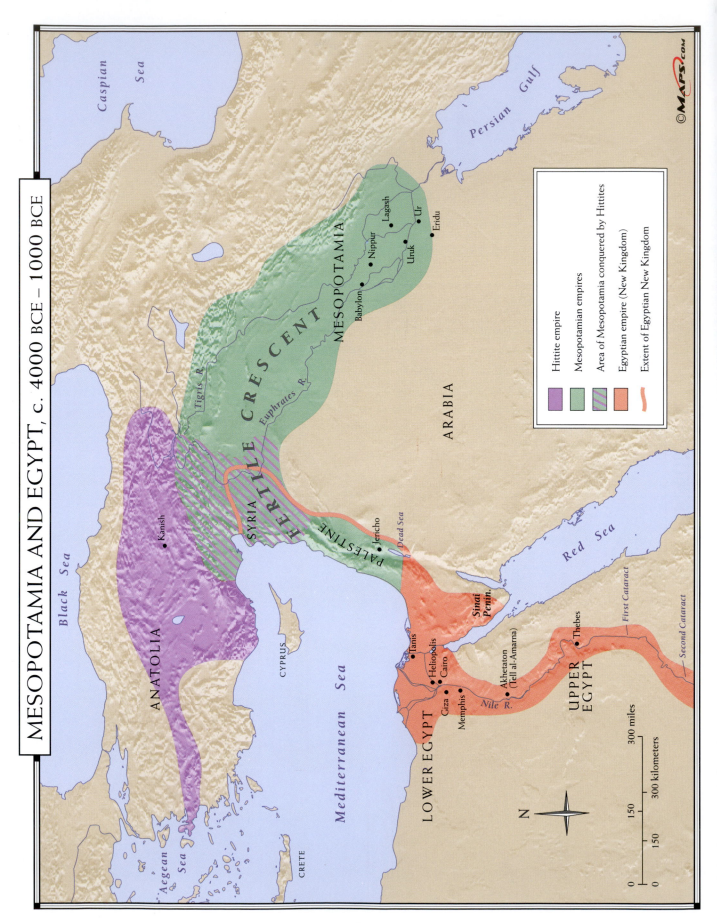

MESOPOTAMIA AND EGYPT, c. 4000 BCE – 1000 BCE

Caspian Sea

Persian Gulf

©MAPS.com

Lagash
Ur
Eridu
Nippur
Uruk
Babylon

MESOPOTAMIA

Tigris R.

Euphrates R.

FERTILE CRESCENT

SYRIA

Kanish

ANATOLIA

Black Sea

Jericho

Dead Sea

PALESTINE

ARABIA

CYPRUS

Mediterranean Sea

Red Sea

Sinai Penin.

First Cataract

Second Cataract

Tanis
Heliopolis
Cairo
Giza
Memphis
Akhetaton (Tell al-Amarna)
Nile R.

LOWER EGYPT

UPPER EGYPT

Thebes

CRETE

Aegean Sea

Legend:
- Hittite empire
- Mesopotamian empires
- Area of Mesopotamia conquered by Hittites
- Egyptian empire (New Kingdom)
- Extent of Egyptian New Kingdom

N

300 miles

300 kilometers

150

150

0

0

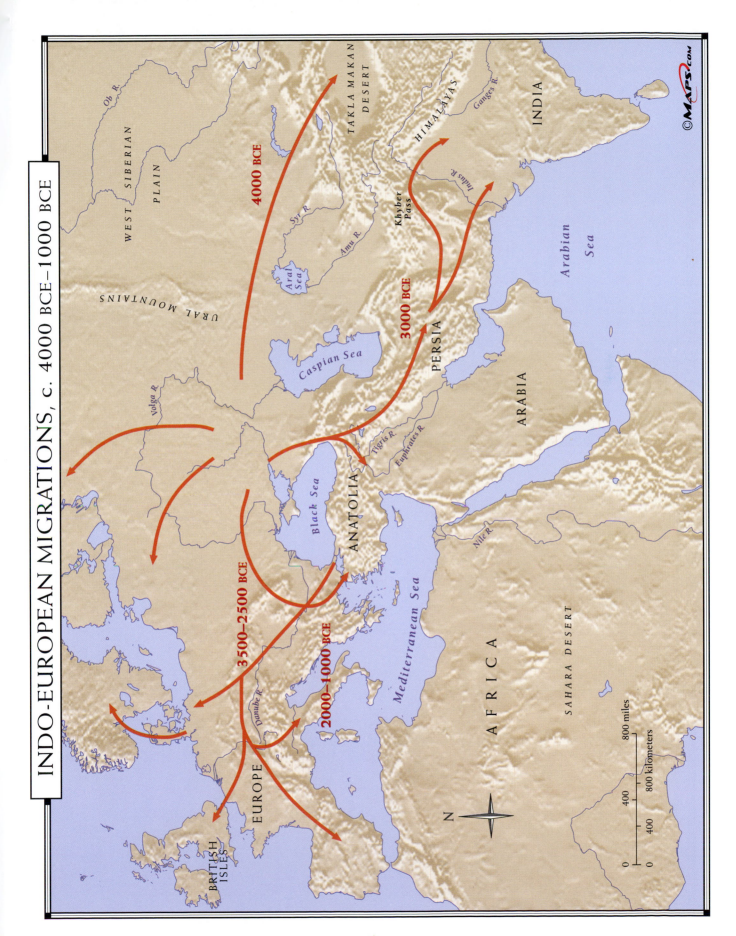

INDO-EUROPEAN MIGRATIONS, c. 4000 BCE–1000 BCE

WEST SIBERIAN PLAIN

URAL MOUNTAINS

TAKLA MAKAN DESERT

HIMALAYAS

INDIA

Ob R.

Syr R.

Amu R.

Aral Sea

Ganges R.

Indus R.

Khyber Pass

4000 BCE

3000 BCE

PERSIA

Arabian Sea

ARABIA

Caspian Sea

Volga R.

Tigris R.

Euphrates R.

Black Sea

ANATOLIA

Mediterranean Sea

Nile R.

AFRICA

SAHARA DESERT

3500–2500 BCE

2000–1000 BCE

Danube R.

EUROPE

BRITISH ISLES

N

800 miles

800 kilometers

400

400

800 miles

800 kilometers

0

0

©MAPS.com

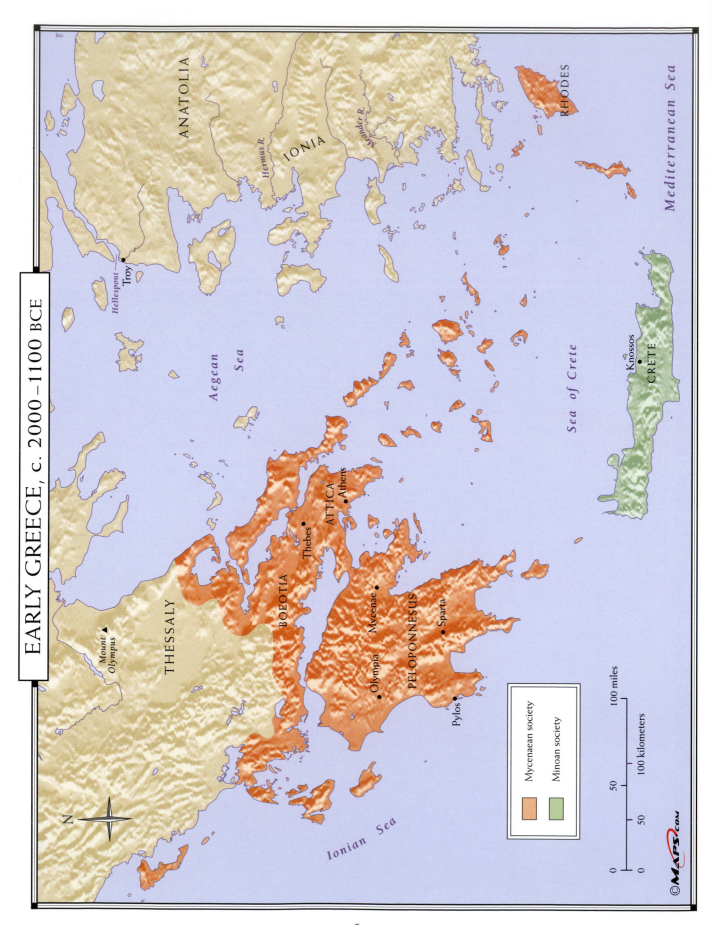

EARLY GREECE, c. 2000–1100 BCE

ANATOLIA

IONIA

Hermus R.

Meander R.

RHODES

Mediterranean Sea

Troy
Hellespont

Aegean Sea

Sea of Crete

Knossos
CRETE

Mount Olympus

THESSALY

BOEOTIA

Thebes

ATTICA
Athens

Mycenae

Olympia
PELOPONNESUS
Sparta

Pylos

Ionian Sea

N

Mycenaean society

Minoan society

100 miles

100 kilometers

50

50

0

0

©MAPS.com

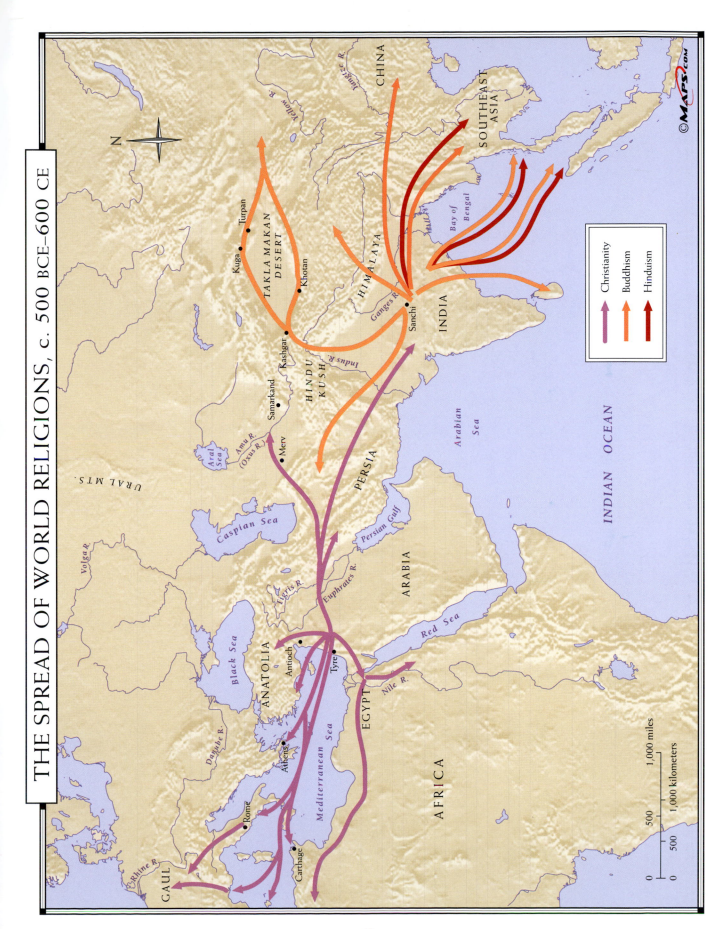

THE SPREAD OF WORLD RELIGIONS, c. 500 BCE–600 CE

Legend:
- Christianity
- Buddhism
- Hinduism

CHINA

SOUTHEAST ASIA

TAKLA MAKAN DESERT

Turpan

Kuga

Khotan

HIMALAYA

Bay of Bengal

INDIA

Ganges R.

Sanchi

Indus R.

Kashgar

HINDU KUSH

Samarkand

Amu R. (Oxus R.)

Merv

Aral Sea

URAL MTS.

Volga R.

Caspian Sea

PERSIA

Arabian Sea

INDIAN OCEAN

ARABIA

Tigris R.

Euphrates R.

Persian Gulf

Red Sea

Nile R.

Black Sea

ANATOLIA

Antioch

Tyre

EGYPT

AFRICA

Danube R.

Athens

Mediterranean Sea

Rome

Carthage

Rhine R.

GAUL

Yellow R.

Yangtze R.

N

©MAPS.com

1,000 miles

1,000 kilometers

500

500

0

0

CLASSICAL GREECE, c. 450 BCE

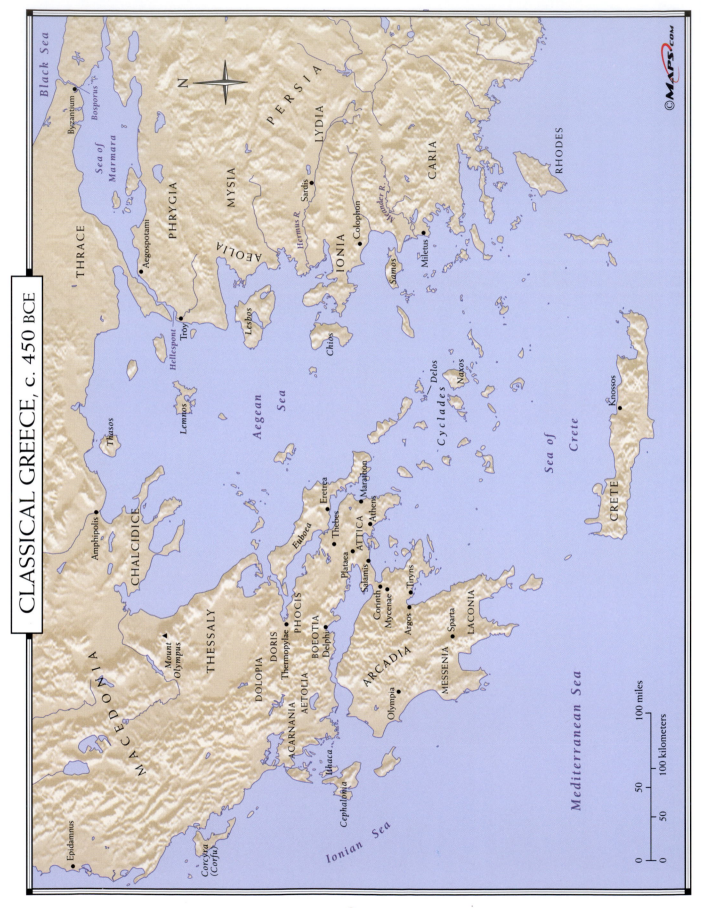

N

Black Sea

Byzantium

Bosporus

Sea of Marmara

THRACE

PERSIA

PHRYGIA

MYSIA

LYDIA

Sardis

Hermus R.

AEOLIA

IONIA

Colophon

CARIA

Maeander R.

RHODES

Aegospotami

Hellespont

Troy

Lesbos

Chios

Samos

Miletus

Lemnos

Thasos

Aegean Sea

Cyclades

Delos

Naxos

Crete

Sea of Crete

Knossos

CRETE

Amphipolis

CHALCIDICE

MACEDONIA

Mount Olympus

THESSALY

DOLOPIA

DORIS

PHOCIS

Thermopylae

AETOLIA

ACARNANIA

BOEOTIA

Delphi

Plataea

Thebes

Eretria

Euboea

Marathon

Athens

ATTICA

Salamis

Corinth

Mycenae

Tiryns

Argos

Sparta

LACONIA

ARCADIA

MESSENIA

Olympia

Ithaca

Cephalonia

Corcyra (Corfu)

Epidamnus

Ionian Sea

Mediterranean Sea

100 miles

100 kilometers

50

50

0

0

ALEXANDER'S EMPIRE, c 323 BCE

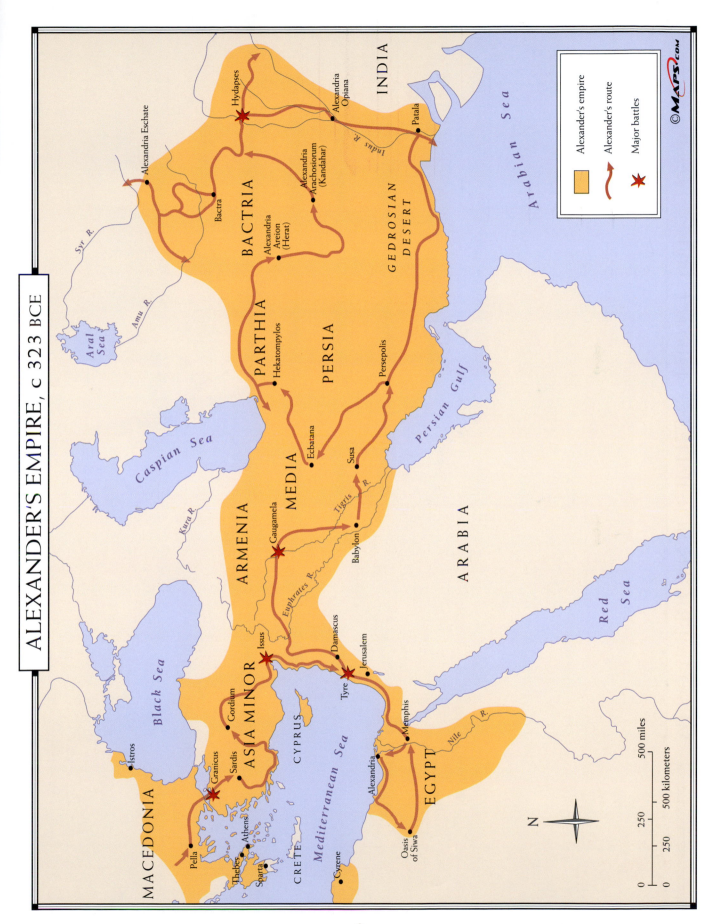

Legend:
- Alexander's empire
- Alexander's route
- Major battles

©MAPS.com

MACEDONIA
Pella
Thebes
Athens
Sparta
Istros
Black Sea
CRETE
Mediterranean Sea
CYPRUS
ASIA MINOR
Granicus
Sardis
Gordium
Cyrene
EGYPT
Alexandria
Memphis
Nile R.
Oasis of Siwa
Jerusalem
Tyre
Damascus
Issus
ARMENIA
Gaugamela
MEDIA
Ecbatana
Babylon
Euphrates R.
Tigris R.
Susa
Persepolis
PERSIA
PARTHIA
Hekatompylos
Caspian Sea
Kura R.
Aral Sea
Amu R.
Syr R.
Alexandria Eschate
Bactria
BACTRIA
Alexandria Areion (Herat)
Alexandria Arachosiorum (Kandahar)
GEDROSIAN DESERT
Hydapses
Alexandria Opiana
INDIA
Indus R.
Patala
Arabian Sea
Persian Gulf
ARABIA
Red Sea

N

500 miles
500 kilometers
0   250   500
0   250   500

MESOAMERICAN SOCIETIES, c. 1200 BCE–900 CE

Caribbean Sea

Gulf of Mexico

PACIFIC OCEAN

MAYA
300 BCE–900 CE

Yucatan Peninsula

Chichen Itzá
• Mayapan
Uxmal •

Tikal •
Yaxchilán •
Palenque •

Copán •

SIERRA MADRE

OLMECS
1200 BCE–400 BCE

La Venta •
San Lorenzo •
Tres Zapotes •

ZAPOTECS
500 BCE–750 CE

Monte Alban •

SIERRA MADRE DEL SUR

TEOTIHUACÁN
100 BCE–750 CE

Tula •
Teotihuacán •
Lake Texcoco

SIERRA MADRE ORIENTAL

N

200 miles
200 kilometers
100
100
0
0

©MAPS.com

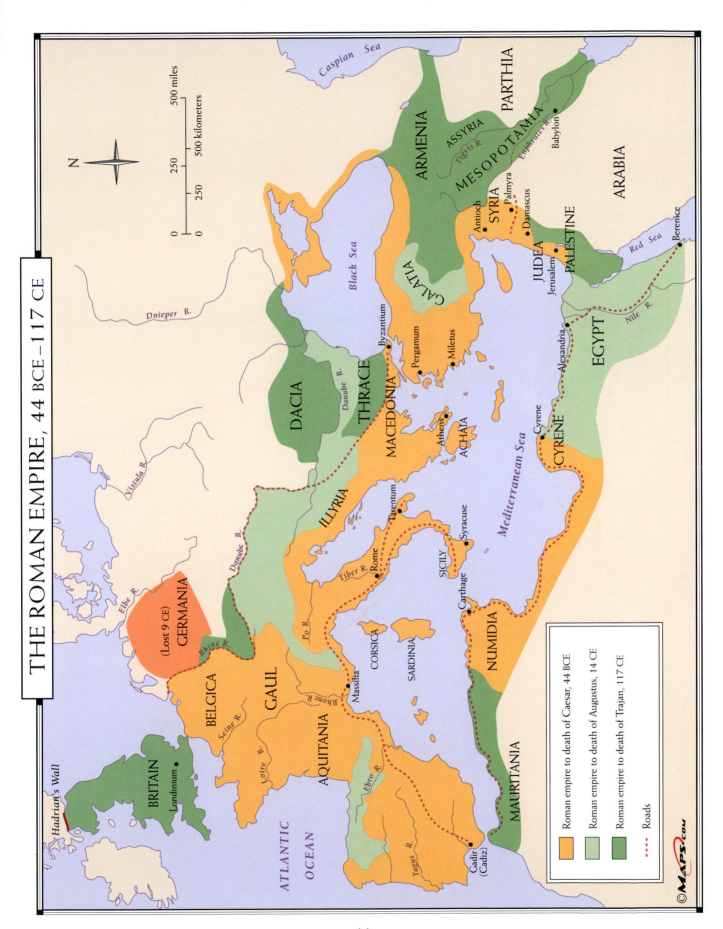

THE ROMAN EMPIRE, 44 BCE–117 CE

Legend:
- Roman empire to death of Caesar, 44 BCE
- Roman empire to death of Augustus, 14 CE
- Roman empire to death of Trajan, 117 CE
- Roads

Caspian Sea

PARTHIA

ARMENIA

ASSYRIA

MESOPOTAMIA

Tigris R.

Euphrates R.

Babylon

ARABIA

GALATIA

SYRIA

Antioch

Palmyra

Damascus

PALESTINE

JUDEA

Jerusalem

Red Sea

Berenice

Nile R.

Alexandria

EGYPT

Black Sea

Dnieper R.

Byzantium

Pergamum

Miletus

DACIA

Danube R.

THRACE

MACEDONIA

Athens

ACHAIA

Cyrene

CYRENE

Mediterranean Sea

Vistula R.

ILLYRIA

Danube R.

Tarentum

Rome

Tiber R.

SICILY

Syracuse

Carthage

NUMIDIA

CORSICA

SARDINIA

GERMANIA
(Lost 9 CE)

Elbe R.

Rhine R.

BELGICA

GAUL

Seine R.

Po R.

Massilia

Rhone R.

AQUITANIA

Loire R.

Ebro R.

Tagus R.

Gadir
(Cadiz)

MAURITANIA

BRITAIN

Londinium

Hadrian's Wall

ATLANTIC
OCEAN

N

500 miles

500 kilometers

250

250

0

0

©Maps.com

— 11 —

MAJOR STATES AND CULTURES OF THE WORLD, c. 100 CE

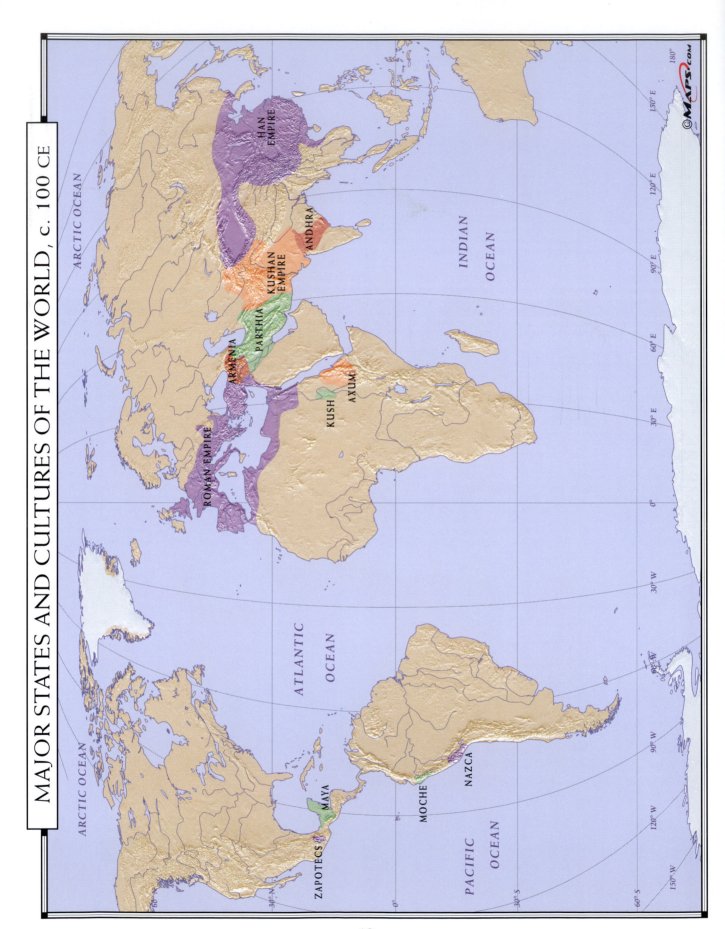

ARCTIC OCEAN

HAN EMPIRE

ANDHRA

KUSHAN EMPIRE

PARTHIA

ARMENIA

ROMAN EMPIRE

KUSH

AXUM

INDIAN OCEAN

ATLANTIC OCEAN

ARCTIC OCEAN

PACIFIC OCEAN

MAYA

ZAPOTECS

MOCHE

NAZCA

180°

150° E

120° E

90° E

60° E

30° E

0°

30° W

90° W

120° W

150° W

60° N

30° N

0°

30° S

60° S

THE ROMAN EMPIRE AND GERMANIC MIGRATIONS, c. 400 CE

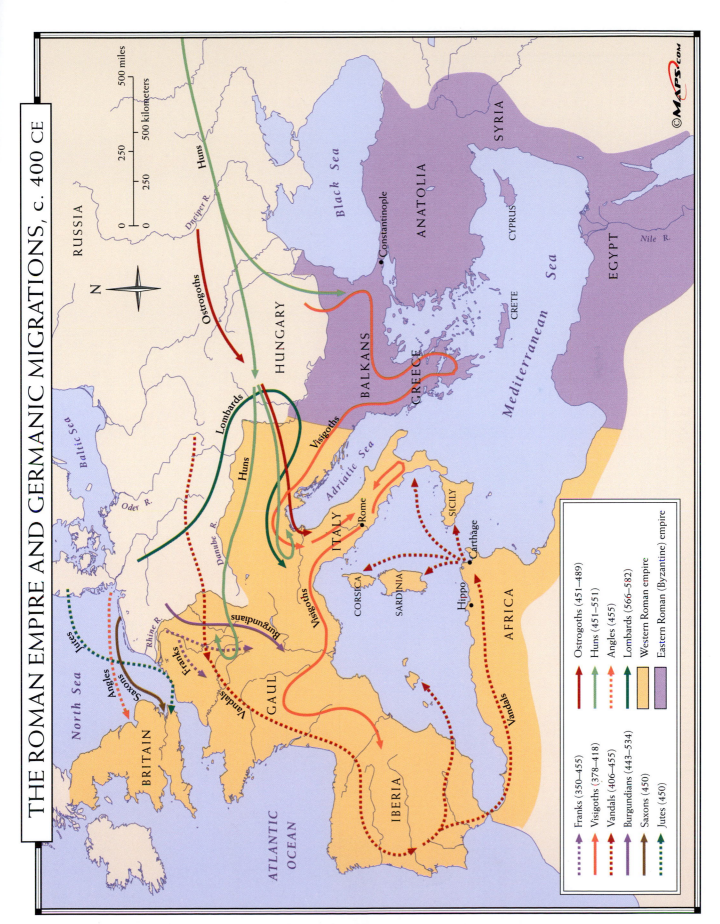

RUSSIA

Black Sea

ANATOLIA

SYRIA

Constantinople

CYPRUS

EGYPT

Nile R.

Mediterranean Sea

CRETE

HUNGARY

BALKANS

GREECE

Adriatic Sea

ITALY

Rome

SICILY

CORSICA

SARDINIA

Carthage

Hippo

AFRICA

Baltic Sea

Oder R.

Danube R.

Rhine R.

North Sea

BRITAIN

ATLANTIC OCEAN

GAUL

IBERIA

Dnieper R.

Huns

Ostrogoths

Lombards

Visigoths

Huns

Burgundians

Franks

Vandals

Visigoths

Jutes

Angles

Saxons

Vandals

500 miles

500 kilometers

0   250   500

0   250   500

N

©MAPS.com

Legend

Franks (350–455)	Ostrogoths (451–489)
Visigoths (378–418)	Huns (451–551)
Vandals (406–455)	Angles (455)
Burgundians (443–534)	Lombards (566–582)
Saxons (450)	Western Roman empire
Jutes (450)	Eastern Roman (Byzantine) empire

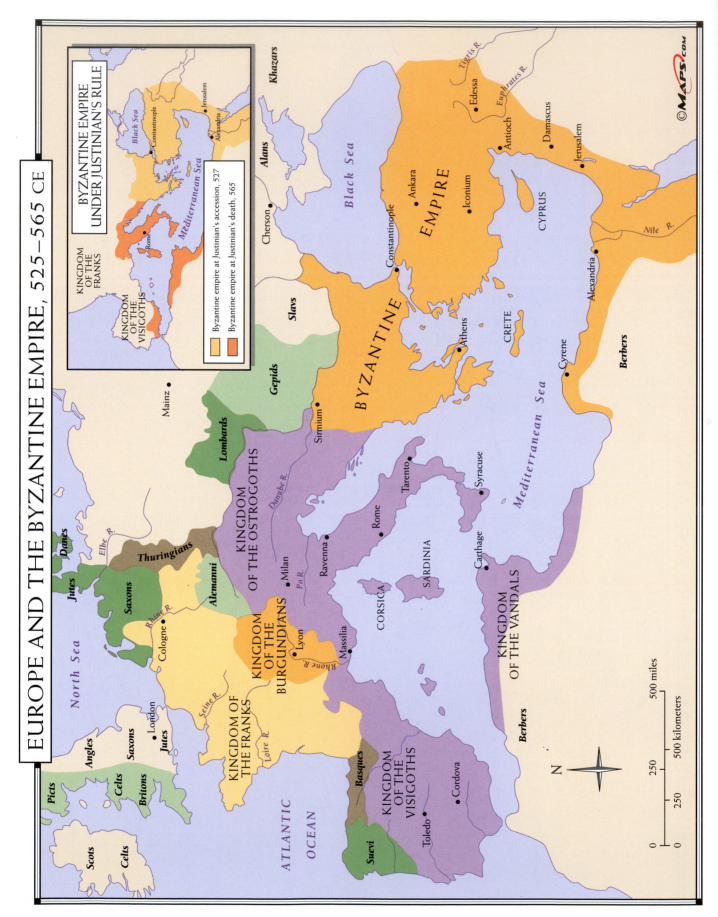

EUROPE AND THE BYZANTINE EMPIRE, 525–565 CE

BYZANTINE EMPIRE UNDER JUSTINIAN'S RULE

KINGDOM OF THE FRANKS

KINGDOM OF THE VISIGOTHS

Mediterranean Sea

Black Sea

Constantinople

Rome

Alexandria

Jerusalem

Byzantine empire at Justinian's accession, 527

Byzantine empire at Justinian's death, 565

Khazars

Alans

Slavs

Gepids

Lombards

Tigris R.

Euphrates R.

Edessa

Damascus

Antioch

Jerusalem

Ankara

BYZANTINE EMPIRE

Iconium

CYPRUS

Nile R.

Black Sea

Constantinople

Cherson

BYZANTINE

Athens

CRETE

Alexandria

Cyrene

Berbers

Mediterranean Sea

Sirmium

Danube R.

Mainz

KINGDOM OF THE OSTROGOTHS

Milan

Po R.

Ravenna

Rome

Tarento

Syracuse

SARDINIA

CORSICA

Carthage

KINGDOM OF THE VANDALS

Berbers

Thuringians

Elbe R.

Danes

Jutes

Saxons

Alemanni

Rhine R.

Cologne

KINGDOM OF THE BURGUNDIANS

Lyon

Massilia

Rhone R.

North Sea

London

Jutes

Saxons

Angles

Picts

Celts

Britons

Scots

Celts

KINGDOM OF THE FRANKS

Seine R.

Loire R.

ATLANTIC OCEAN

Basques

KINGDOM OF THE VISIGOTHS

Cordova

Toledo

Suevi

500 miles

500 kilometers

250

250

0

0

N

– 14 –

TRADE ROUTES IN THE INDIAN OCEAN, c. 500–1000 CE

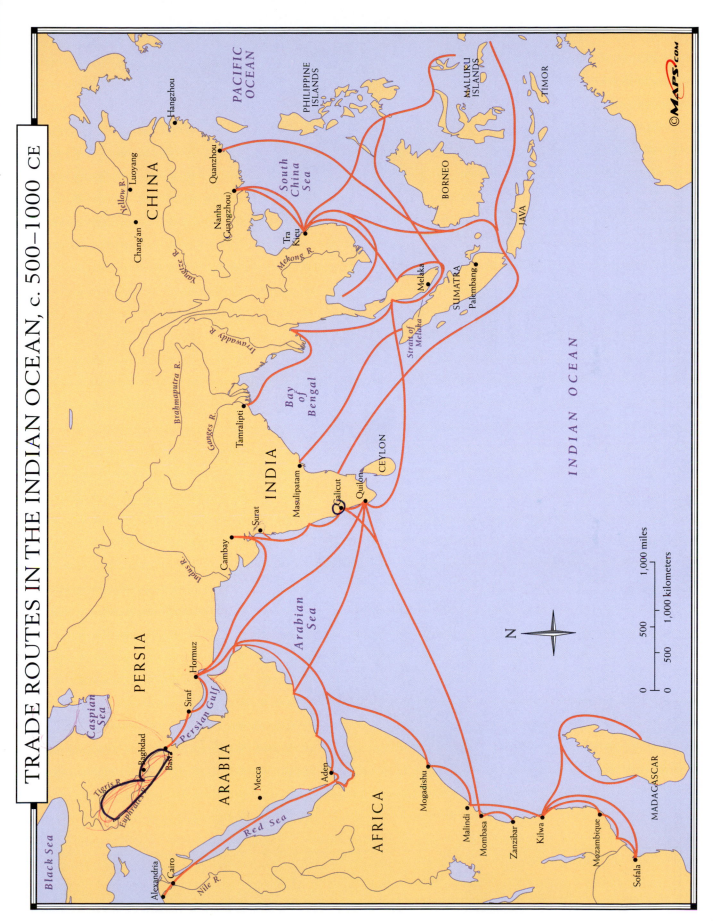

Black Sea

Caspian Sea

PERSIA

Tigris R.
Euphrates R.
Baghdad
Basra
Siraf
Hormuz
Persian Gulf

ARABIA
Mecca
Red Sea
Aden

Alexandria
Cairo
Nile R.

AFRICA
Mogadishu
Malindi
Mombasa
Zanzibar
Kilwa
Mozambique
Sofala

MADAGASCAR

INDIA
Cambay
Surat
Masulipatam
Tamralipti
Calicut
Quilon
CEYLON

Arabian Sea

Bay of Bengal

INDIAN OCEAN

Indus R.
Brahmaputra R.
Ganges R.
Irrawaddy R.

CHINA
Yellow R.
Luoyang
Chang'an
Yangtze R.
Hangzhou
Quanzhou
Nanha (Guangzhou)
Tra Kieu
Mekong R.

South China Sea

PACIFIC OCEAN

PHILIPPINE ISLANDS

MALUKU ISLANDS
TIMOR

BORNEO
SUMATRA
Melaka
Strait of Melaka
Palembang
JAVA

N

1,000 miles
500
0

1,000 kilometers
500
0

©MAPS.com

— 15 —

THE SPREAD OF ISLAM, 622 – 750 CE

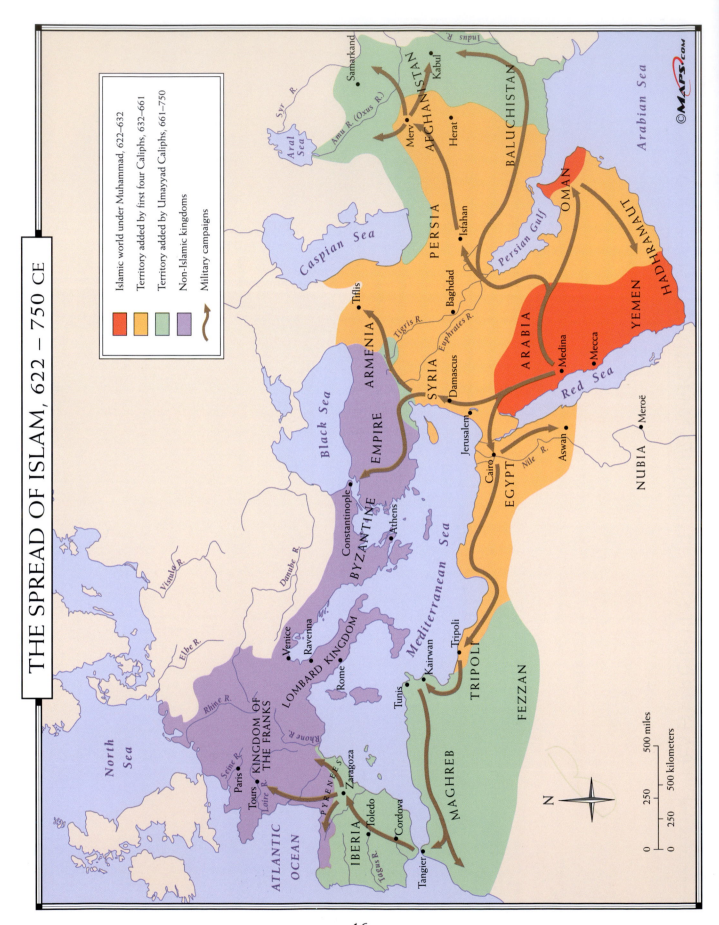

Legend:
- Islamic world under Muhammad, 622–632
- Territory added by first four Caliphs, 632–661
- Territory added by Umayyad Caliphs, 661–750
- Non-Islamic kingdoms
- Military campaigns

©MAPS.com

ATLANTIC OCEAN
North Sea
IBERIA
Tagus R.
Toledo
Cordova
Tangier
Zaragoza
Paris
Tours
Loire R.
Seine R.
KINGDOM OF THE FRANKS
PYRENEES
Rhine R.
Rhône R.
Elbe R.
Vistula R.
Danube R.
Venice
Ravenna
Rome
LOMBARD KINGDOM
Black Sea
Constantinople
Athens
BYZANTINE EMPIRE
ARMENIA
Tiflis
Caspian Sea
Aral Sea
Syr R.
Amu R. (Oxus R.)
Samarkand
Kabul
Indus R.
AFGHANISTAN
Herat
Merv
BALUCHISTAN
PERSIA
Isfahan
Baghdad
Tigris R.
Euphrates R.
Persian Gulf
OMAN
Arabian Sea
HADHRAMAUT
YEMEN
ARABIA
Medina
Mecca
Red Sea
SYRIA
Damascus
Jerusalem
Cairo
EGYPT
Nile R.
Aswan
NUBIA
Meroë
Mediterranean Sea
Tripoli
TRIPOLI
Kairwan
Tunis
FEZZAN
MAGHREB

N

0   250   500 miles
0   250   500 kilometers

– 16 –

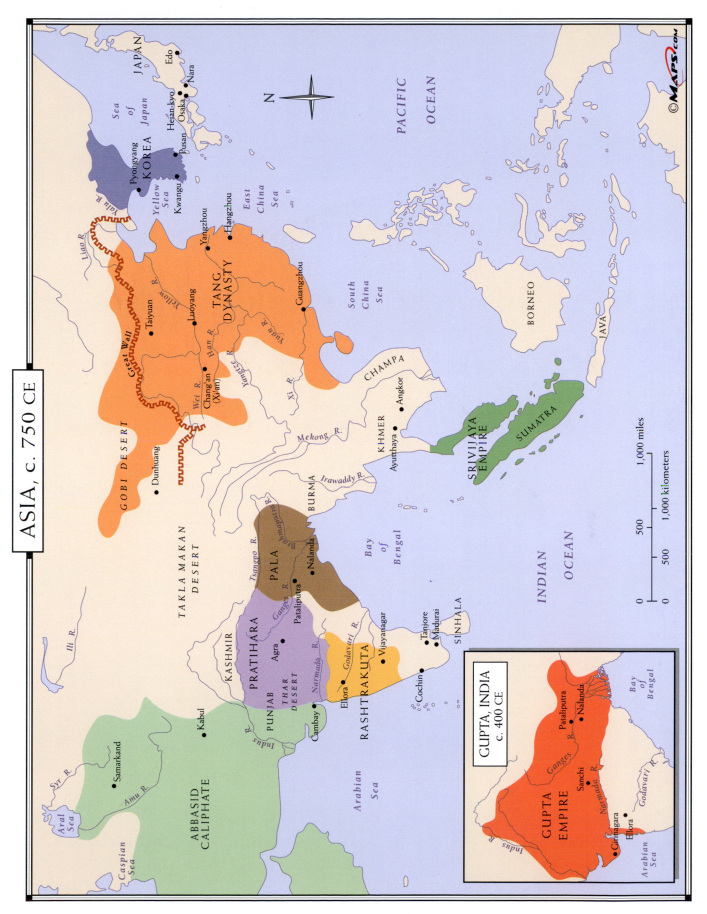

ASIA, c. 750 CE

JAPAN
- Edo
- Nara
- Heian-kyo
- Osaka

Sea of Japan

KOREA
- Pyongyang
- Kwangju
- Pusan

Yellow Sea

East China Sea

N

PACIFIC OCEAN

Yalu R.

Liao R.

Great Wall

TANG DYNASTY
- Taiyuan
- Luoyang
- Yangzhou
- Hangzhou
- Guangzhou
- Chang'an (Xi'an)
- Dunhuang

GOBI DESERT

Yellow R.

Han R.

Wei R.

Yuan R.

Xi R.

Yangtze R.

South China Sea

CHAMPA

BORNEO

JAVA

SUMATRA

SRIVIJAYA EMPIRE

TAKLA MAKAN DESERT

Mekong R.

Irawaddy R.

KHMER
- Angkor
- Ayutthaya

BURMA

Brahmaputra

Tsangpo R.

PALA
- Nalanda
- Pataliputra

Ganges R.

Bay of Bengal

PRATIHARA
- Agra

KASHMIR

PUNJAB

THAR DESERT

Narmada R.

Godavari R.

RASHTRAKUTA
- Ellora
- Vijayanagar
- Cochin
- Tanjore
- Madurai

SINHALA

INDIAN OCEAN

- Cambay

Indus R.

ABBASID CALIPHATE
- Kabul
- Samarkand

Syr R.

Amu R.

Aral Sea

Caspian Sea

Ili R.

Arabian Sea

Scale:
1,000 miles
1,000 kilometers
500
500
0
0

GUPTA, INDIA c. 400 CE

GUPTA EMPIRE
- Pataliputra
- Nalanda
- Sanchi
- Girinagara
- Ellora

Ganges R.

Narmada R.

Godavari R.

Indus R.

Bay of Bengal

Arabian Sea

©MAPS.com

— 17 —

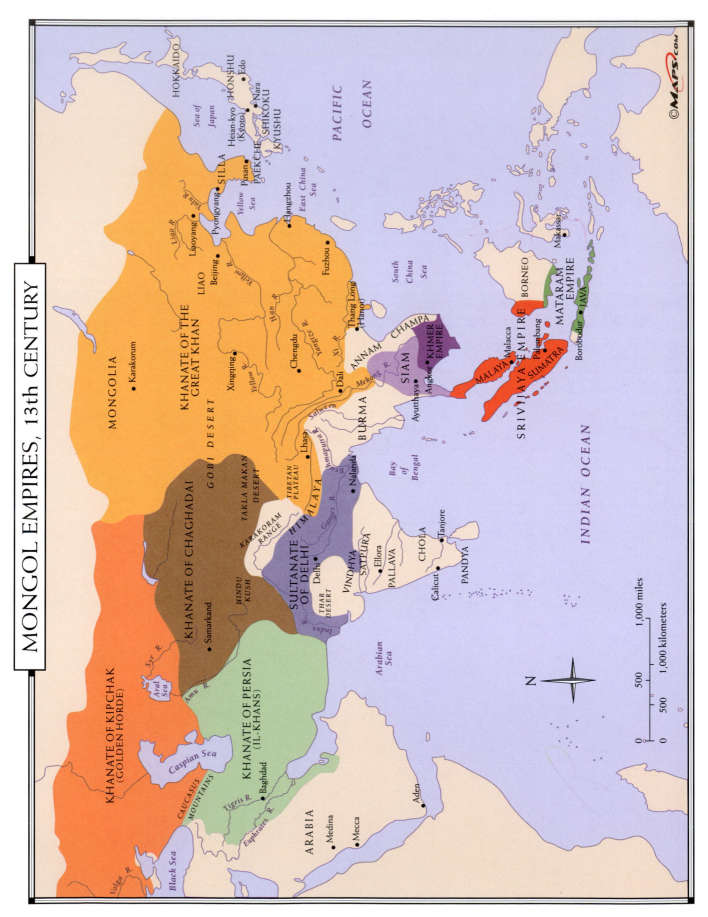

MONGOL EMPIRES, 13th CENTURY

HOKKAIDO

HONSHU

Sea of
Japan

Edo

Heian-kyo
(Kyoto)

Nara

PACIFIC
OCEAN

SHIKOKU

KYUSHU

PAEKCHE

Pusan

SILLA

Pyongyang

Yellow
Sea

East China
Sea

Liao R.

Yalu R.

Liaoyang

LIAO

Hangzhou

Yangzhou

Beijing

Yellow R.

Fuzhou

MONGOLIA

KHANATE OF THE
GREAT KHAN

Karakorum

Han R.

South
China
Sea

GOBI DESERT

Xingqing

Chengdu

Yangtze R.

BORNEO

Yellow R.

Xi R.

Thang Long
(Hanoi)

MATARAM
EMPIRE

Dali

Mekong R.

ANNAM

CHAMPA

SRIVIJAYA EMPIRE

Makassar

JAVA

Borobudur

TAKLA MAKAN
DESERT

Salween R.

KHMER
EMPIRE

Palembang

Lhasa

SIAM

Angkor

MALACCA

MALAYA

SUMATRA

TIBETAN
PLATEAU

Brahmaputra R.

BURMA

Ayutthaya

KHANATE OF CHAGHADAI

KARAKORAM
RANGE

HIMALAYA

MALAYA

Nalanda

Bay
of
Bengal

INDIAN OCEAN

Samarkand

HINDU
KUSH

Ganges R.

SULTANATE
OF DELHI

Delhi

VINDHYA

SATPURA

CHOLA

Tanjore

Ellora

PALLAVA

THAR
DESERT

Indus R.

Calicut

PANDYA

KHANATE OF KIPCHAK
(GOLDEN HORDE)

Syr R.

Aral
Sea

Amu R.

KHANATE OF PERSIA
(IL-KHANS)

Arabian
Sea

N

Caspian Sea

Baghdad

CAUCASUS
MOUNTAINS

Tigris R.

Euphrates R.

Aden

Black Sea

ARABIA

Medina

Mecca

Volga R.

1,000 miles

1,000 kilometers

500

500

0

0

©MAPS.com

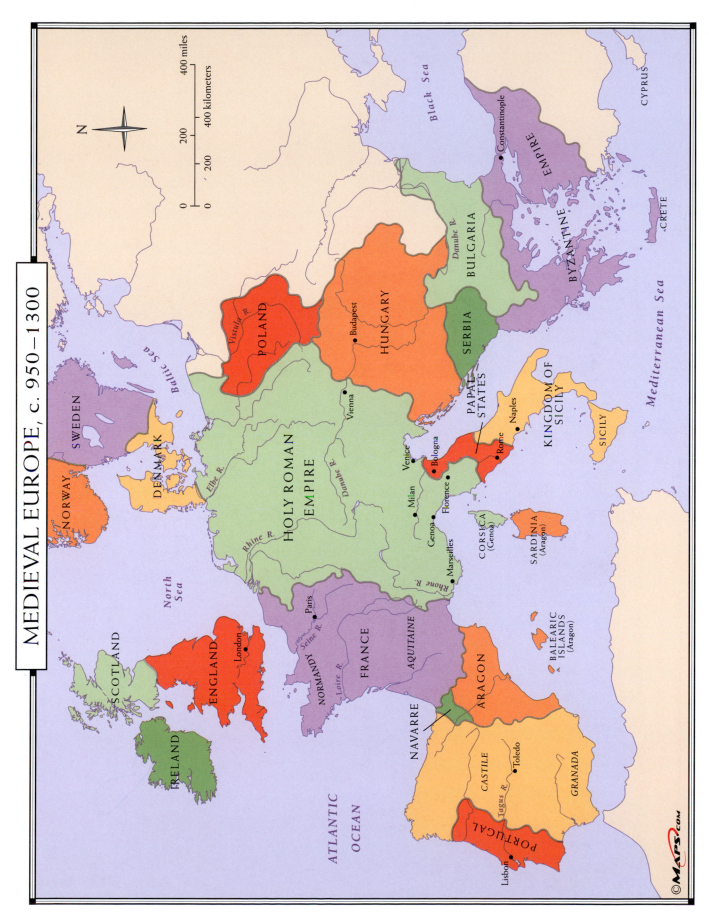

MEDIEVAL EUROPE, c. 950–1300

400 miles
400 kilometers
0   200   400
0   200   400

N

ATLANTIC OCEAN

North Sea

SCOTLAND

IRELAND

ENGLAND
London

NORWAY

SWEDEN

DENMARK

Baltic Sea

POLAND
Vistula R.

HOLY ROMAN EMPIRE
Elbe R.
Rhine R.
Danube R.
Vienna

HUNGARY
Budapest
Danube R.

BULGARIA

SERBIA

BYZANTINE EMPIRE
Constantinople

Black Sea

CYPRUS

CRETE

Mediterranean Sea

NORMANDY
Paris
Seine R.
Loire R.
FRANCE
AQUITAINE
Rhône R.
Marseilles

Milan
Genoa
Venice
Florence
Bologna
PAPAL STATES
Rome
Naples
KINGDOM OF SICILY
SICILY

CORSICA
(Genoa)
SARDINIA
(Aragon)

BALEARIC ISLANDS
(Aragon)

NAVARRE
ARAGON
CASTILE
Toledo
Tagus R.
GRANADA
PORTUGAL
Lisbon

©MAPS.com

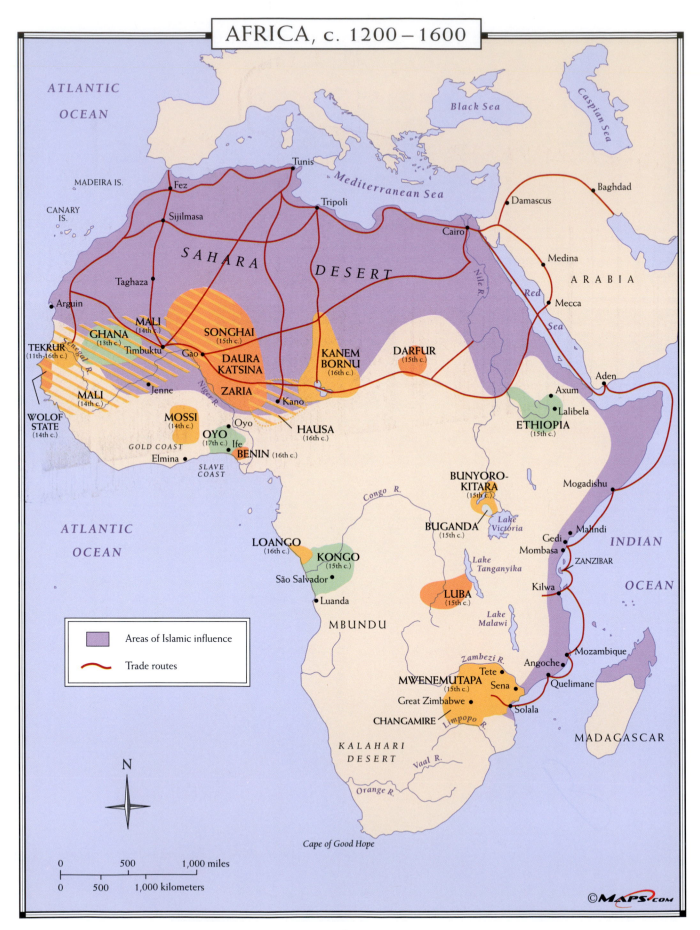

AFRICA, c. 1200–1600

ATLANTIC OCEAN

Black Sea

Caspian Sea

MADEIRA IS.

CANARY IS.

Mediterranean Sea

Tunis

Fez

Sijilmasa

Tripoli

Cairo

Damascus

Baghdad

Medina

ARABIA

SAHARA   DESERT

Nile R.

Red Sea

Mecca

Taghaza

Arguin

GHANA (13th c.)

MALI (14th c.)

SONGHAI (15th c.)

Timbuktu

Gao

DAURA KATSINA

KANEM BORNU (16th c.)

DARFUR (15th c.)

Aden

Axum

Lalibela

TEKRUR (11th–16th c.)

Senegal R.

Jenne

ZARIA

Niger R.

Kano

ETHIOPIA (15th c.)

MALI (14th c.)

WOLOF STATE (14th c.)

MOSSI (14th c.)

Oyo

HAUSA (16th c.)

OYO (17th c.)

Ife

GOLD COAST

Elmina

BENIN (16th c.)

SLAVE COAST

BUNYORO-KITARA (15th c.)

Mogadishu

Congo R.

BUGANDA (15th c.)

Lake Victoria

Malindi

Gedi

INDIAN

LOANGO (16th c.)

KONGO (15th c.)

Mombasa

ZANZIBAR

São Salvador

Lake Tanganyika

LUBA (15th c.)

Kilwa

OCEAN

Luanda

MBUNDU

Lake Malawi

Zambezi R.

Mozambique

Angoche

Tete

Quelimane

MWENEMUTAPA (15th c.)

Sena

Great Zimbabwe

Solala

CHANGAMIRE

Limpopo R.

MADAGASCAR

KALAHARI DESERT

Vaal R.

Orange R.

N

Cape of Good Hope

Areas of Islamic influence

Trade routes

| 0 | 500 | 1,000 miles |
| 0 | 500 | 1,000 kilometers |

©Maps.com

SOUTH AMERICAN STATES, 500–1532 CE

N

Caribbean Sea

ATLANTIC OCEAN

Quito

Amazon R.

Ucayali R.

CHIMU
800–1465 CE

Chimu

INCA EMPIRE
1438–1532 CE

▲ *Machu Picchu*

Cuzco

Lake Titicaca

Puno
Copacabana • Tiahuanaco

TIAHUANACO
500–1000 CE

Paraguay R.

PACIFIC OCEAN

San Pedro de Atacama

INCA EMPIRE
1438–1532 CE

ATLANTIC OCEAN

Coquimbo

Parana R.

Talca

| 0 | 300 | 600 miles |
| 0 | 300 | 600 kilometers |

©MAPS.com

ANDES

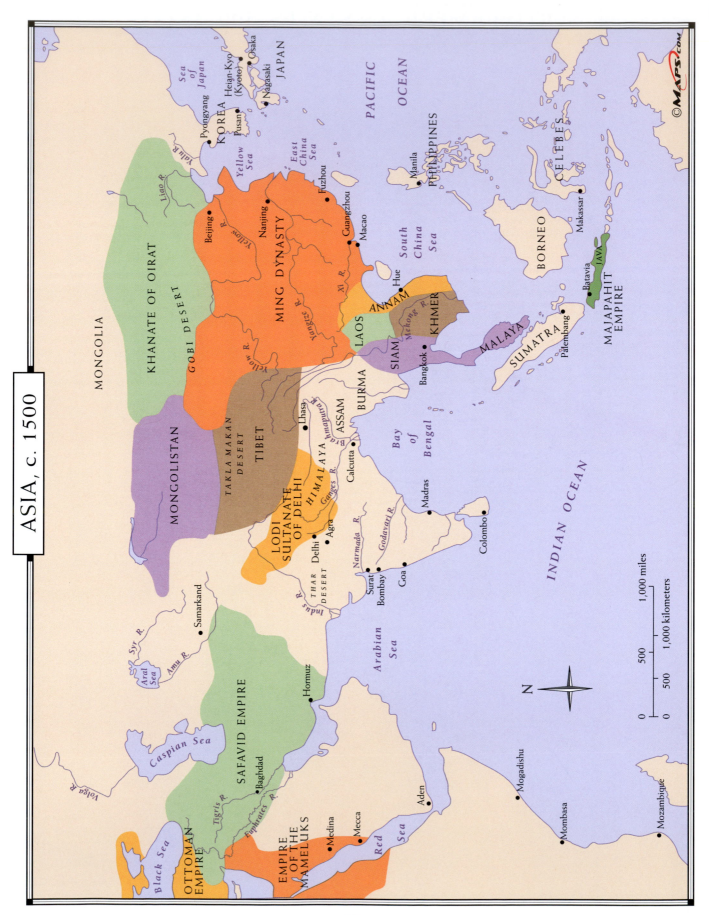

ASIA, c. 1500

MONGOLIA

KHANATE OF OIRAT

GOBI DESERT

MING DYNASTY

MONGOLISTAN

TAKLA MAKAN DESERT

TIBET

LODI SULTANATE OF DELHI

HIMALAYA

THAR DESERT

SAFAVID EMPIRE

OTTOMAN EMPIRE

EMPIRE OF THE MAMELUKS

ASSAM

BURMA

LAOS

ANNAM

KHMER

SIAM

MALAYA

SUMATRA

BORNEO

CELEBES

PHILIPPINES

JAVA

MAJAPAHIT EMPIRE

KOREA

JAPAN

Sea of Japan

Yellow Sea

East China Sea

South China Sea

PACIFIC OCEAN

Bay of Bengal

INDIAN OCEAN

Arabian Sea

Red Sea

Caspian Sea

Aral Sea

Black Sea

Heian-Kyo (Kyoto)

Osaka

Nagasaki

Pyongyang

Pusan

Beijing

Nanjing

Fuzhou

Guangzhou

Macao

Hue

Bangkok

Palembang

Batavia

Makassar

Manila

Lhasa

Calcutta

Madras

Colombo

Delhi

Agra

Surat

Bombay

Goa

Samarkand

Hormuz

Baghdad

Medina

Mecca

Aden

Mogadishu

Mombasa

Mozambique

Yalu R.

Liao R.

Yellow R.

Yangtze R.

Xi R.

Mekong R.

Brahmaputra R.

Ganges R.

Narmada R.

Godavari R.

Indus R.

Syr R.

Amu R.

Tigris R.

Euphrates R.

Volga R.

N

1,000 miles

1,000 kilometers

500

500

0

0

©MAPS.com

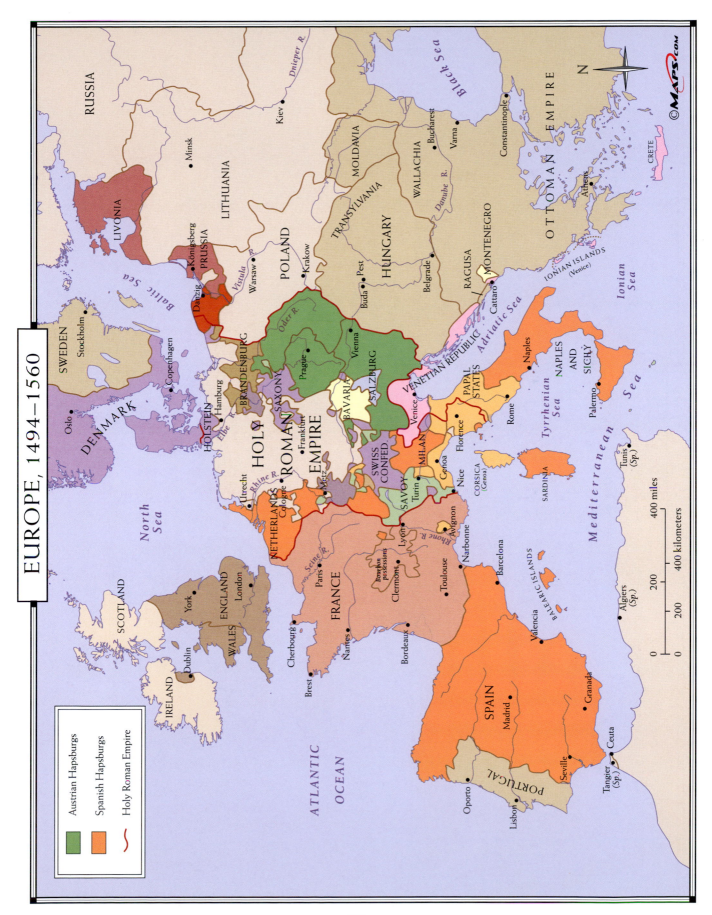

EUROPE, 1494–1560

Legend:
- Austrian Hapsburgs (green)
- Spanish Hapsburgs (orange)
- Holy Roman Empire (red line)

RUSSIA

SWEDEN
- Stockholm

LIVONIA

LITHUANIA
- Minsk

PRUSSIA
- Königsberg
- Danzig

POLAND
- Warsaw
- Krakow

MOLDAVIA

TRANSYLVANIA

WALLACHIA
- Bucharest
- Varna

HUNGARY
- Buda
- Pest
- Belgrade

OTTOMAN EMPIRE
- Constantinople
- Athens

CRETE

Black Sea

Dnieper R.

Kiev

Baltic Sea

Vistula R.

Oder R.

Danube R.

DENMARK
- Oslo
- Copenhagen

HOLSTEIN
- Hamburg

BRANDENBURG

SAXONY

HOLY ROMAN EMPIRE
- Frankfurt
- Prague
- Vienna
- Salzburg

BAVARIA

SWISS CONFED.

Elbe R.

Rhine R.

NETHERLANDS
- Utrecht
- Cologne
- Metz

VENETIAN REPUBLIC
- Venice

RAGUSA

MONTENEGRO
- Cattaro

Adriatic Sea

PAPAL STATES
- Rome
- Florence

MILAN
- Genoa

SAVOY
- Turin
- Nice

NAPLES
- Naples

NAPLES AND SICILY
- Palermo

IONIAN ISLANDS (Venice)

Ionian Sea

Tyrrhenian Sea

CORSICA (Genoa)

SARDINIA

Mediterranean Sea

Tunis (Sp.)

North Sea

SCOTLAND

ENGLAND
- York
- London

WALES

IRELAND
- Dublin

Cherbourg

Brest
- Nantes

FRANCE
- Paris
- Clermont
- Bordeaux
- Toulouse

Bourbon possessions

Lyon
- Avignon
- Narbonne

Rhône R.

Seine R.

ATLANTIC OCEAN

Barcelona

BALEARIC ISLANDS

Valencia

Algiers (Sp.)

SPAIN
- Madrid
- Granada
- Seville

PORTUGAL
- Oporto
- Lisbon

Tangier (Sp.)
Ceuta

©MAPS.com

N

400 miles
400 kilometers
200
0

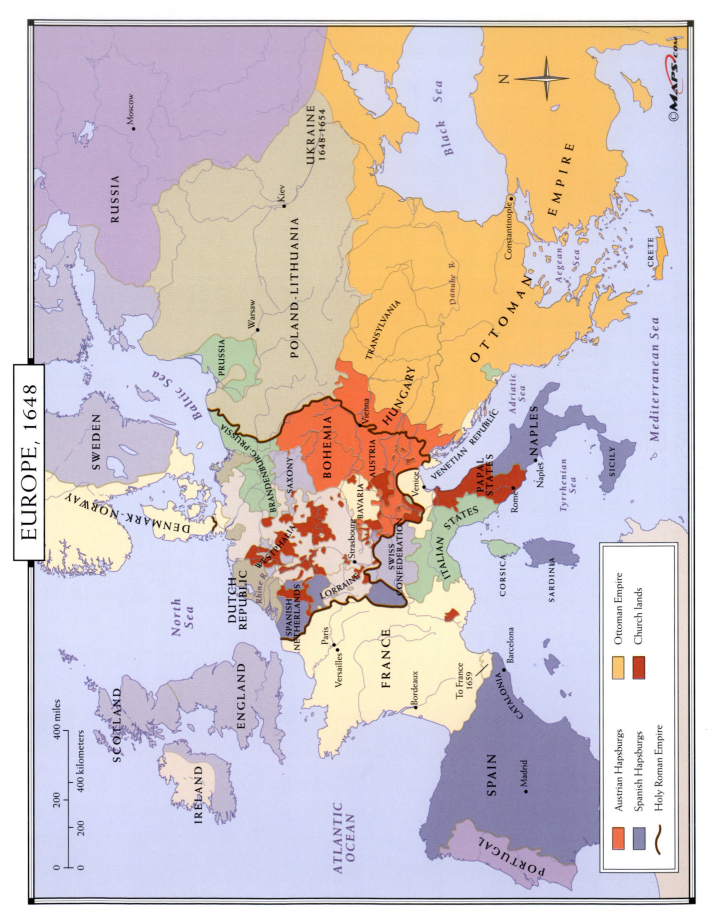

EUROPE, 1648

Legend:
- Austrian Hapsburgs
- Spanish Hapsburgs
- Holy Roman Empire
- Ottoman Empire
- Church lands

RUSSIA
Moscow

SWEDEN

DENMARK-NORWAY

Baltic Sea

POLAND-LITHUANIA
Warsaw
Kiev

UKRAINE 1648-1654

PRUSSIA

BRANDENBURG-PRUSSIA

SAXONY

BOHEMIA

SILESIA

Vienna

AUSTRIA

HUNGARY

TRANSYLVANIA

Danube R.

OTTOMAN EMPIRE

Black Sea

Constantinople

Aegean Sea

CRETE

Mediterranean Sea

Adriatic Sea

VENETIAN REPUBLIC
Venice

PAPAL STATES
Rome

ITALIAN STATES

NAPLES
Naples

Tyrrhenian Sea

SICILY

SARDINIA

CORSICA

SCOTLAND

IRELAND

ENGLAND

North Sea

ATLANTIC OCEAN

DUTCH REPUBLIC

WESTPHALIA

Rhine R.

SPANISH NETHERLANDS

LORRAINE

Strasbourg

BAVARIA

SWISS CONFEDERATION

Paris

Versailles

FRANCE

Bordeaux

To France 1659

CATALONIA
Barcelona

SPAIN
Madrid

PORTUGAL

400 miles
400 kilometers
200
200
0
0

N

©MAPS.com

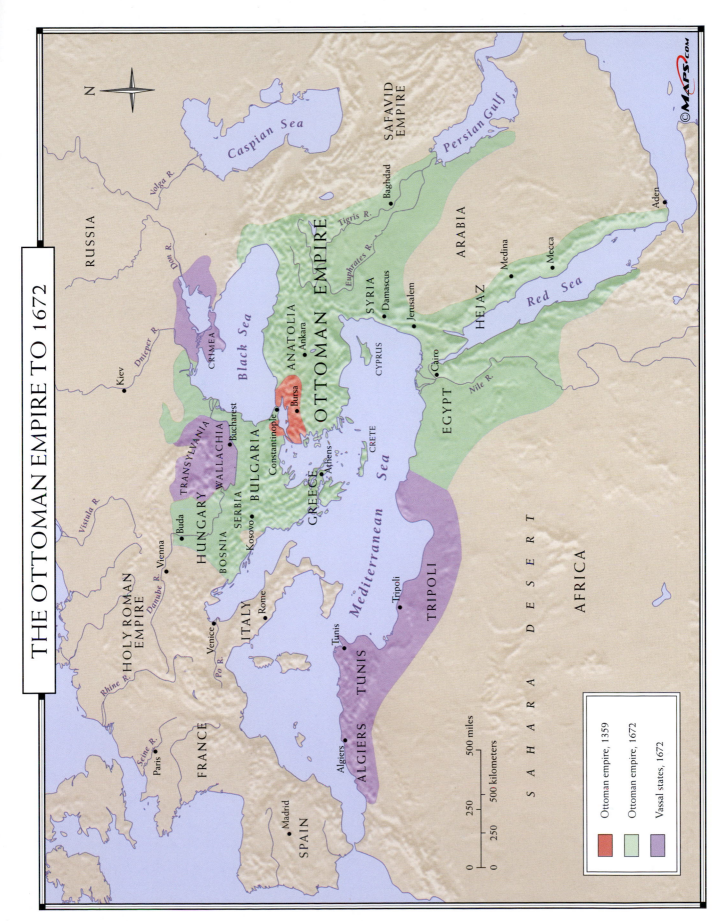

THE OTTOMAN EMPIRE TO 1672

N

RUSSIA

Caspian Sea

SAFAVID EMPIRE

Persian Gulf

Volga R.

Don R.

Dnieper R.

Kiev

Baghdad

Tigris R.

ARABIA

Aden

CRIMEA

Black Sea

OTTOMAN EMPIRE

ANATOLIA

Ankara

Euphrates R.

SYRIA

Damascus

HEJAZ

Medina

Mecca

Red Sea

TRANSYLVANIA

Bucharest

WALLACHIA

Bursa

Constantinople

Jerusalem

Cairo

Nile R.

EGYPT

CYPRUS

Vistula R.

HUNGARY

Buda

Vienna

BOSNIA

SERBIA

Kosovo

BULGARIA

GREECE

Athens

CRETE

Mediterranean Sea

HOLY ROMAN EMPIRE

Danube R.

Rhine R.

ITALY

Venice

Rome

Po R.

Tripoli

TRIPOLI

SAHARA DESERT

AFRICA

Tunis

TUNIS

ALGIERS

Algiers

FRANCE

Seine R.

Paris

Madrid

SPAIN

500 miles

500 kilometers

250

250

0

0

Ottoman empire, 1359

Ottoman empire, 1672

Vassal states, 1672

©MAPS.com

— 25 —

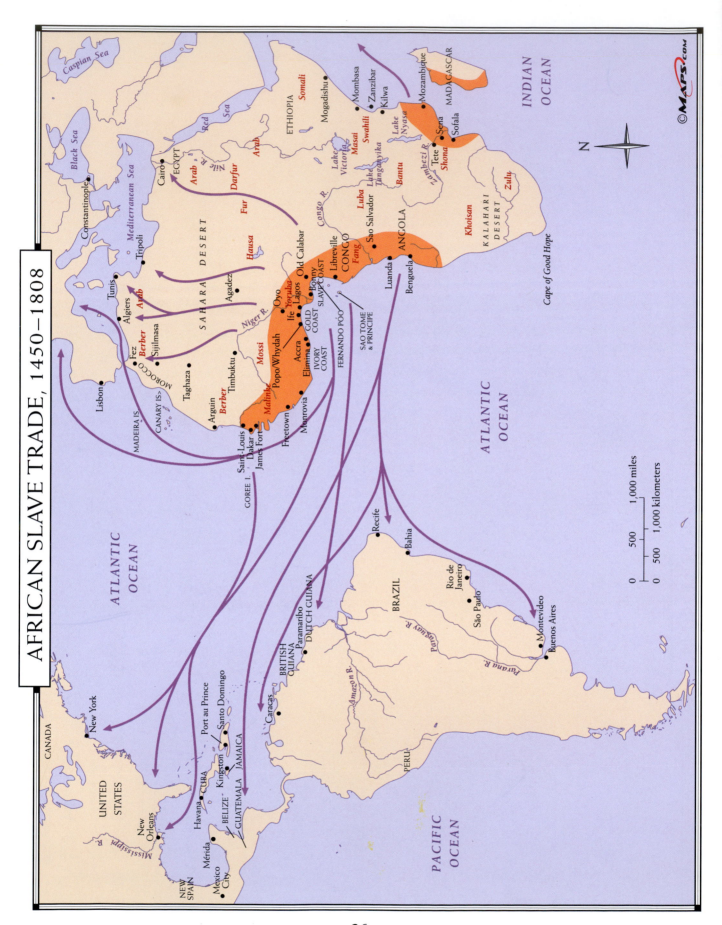

AFRICAN SLAVE TRADE, 1450–1808

INDIAN OCEAN

Caspian Sea

Black Sea

Red Sea

Mediterranean Sea

ATLANTIC OCEAN

PACIFIC OCEAN

Constantinople

Cairo
EGYPT
Arab
Darfur
Fur
ETHIOPIA
Somali
Mogadishu
Mombasa
Zanzibar
Kilwa
Mozambique
MADAGASCAR
Sena
Sofala
Tete
Shona
Zulu
Masai
Swahili
Bantu
Lake Victoria
Lake Tanganyika
Lake Nyasa
Khoisan
KALAHARI DESERT
Cape of Good Hope

Tripoli
Tunis
Algiers
Arab
Berber
Fez
Sijilmasa
MOROCCO
Berber
Taghaza
SAHARA DESERT
Agadez
Hausa
Timbuktu
Niger R.
Mossi
Malinke
Arguin
Saint-Louis
Dakar
James Fort
GOREE I.
Freetown
Monrovia
IVORY COAST
Elmina
Accra
GOLD COAST
Popo/Whydah
Lagos
Bonny
SLAVE COAST
Yoruba
Ife
Oyo
Old Calabar
FERNANDO POO
SAO TOME & PRINCIPE
Libreville
CONGO
Fang
Sao Salvador
Luba
Congo R.
Zambezi R.
ANGOLA
Luanda
Benguela

Lisbon
MADEIRA IS.
CANARY IS.

N

NEW SPAIN
Mexico City
Mérida
Mississippi R.
New Orleans
UNITED STATES
New York
CANADA
Havana
CUBA
BELIZE
GUATEMALA
Kingston
JAMAICA
Port au Prince
Santo Domingo
Caracas
PERU
BRITISH GUIANA
Paramaribo
DUTCH GUIANA
Amazon R.
BRAZIL
Recife
Bahia
Rio de Janeiro
São Paulo
Paraguay R.
Paraná R.
Montevideo
Buenos Aires

ATLANTIC OCEAN

©MAPS.com

1,000 miles
500
0
1,000 kilometers
500
0

— 26 —

EXPLORATION AND COLONIZATION, c. 1700

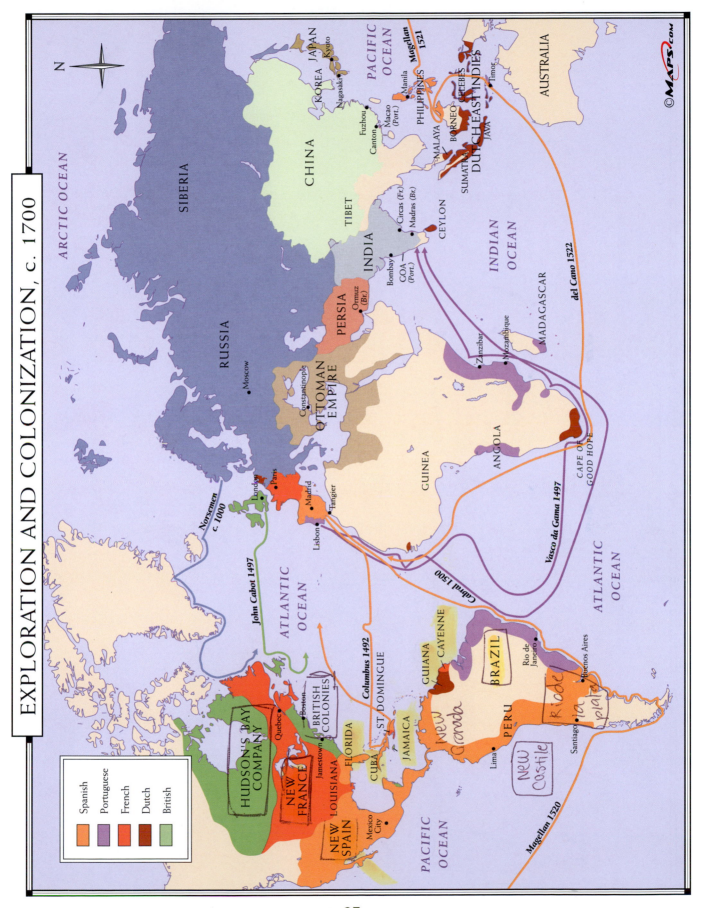

Legend:
- Spanish
- Portuguese
- French
- Dutch
- British

ARCTIC OCEAN

SIBERIA

RUSSIA
- Moscow

CHINA
- Fuzhou
- Canton

JAPAN
- Kyoto
- Nagasaki

KOREA

TIBET

INDIA
- Bombay
- GOA (Port.)
- Madras (Br.)
- Circas (Fr.)

PERSIA
- Ormuz (Br.)

OTTOMAN EMPIRE
- Constantinople

CEYLON

PHILIPPINES
- Manila
- Macao (Port.)

BORNEO
- CELEBES
- MALAYA
- SUMATRA
- JAVA
- Timor

DUTCH EAST INDIES

AUSTRALIA

PACIFIC OCEAN

Magellan 1521

del Cano 1522

INDIAN OCEAN

MADAGASCAR
- Zanzibar
- Mozambique

ANGOLA

GUINEA

Vasca da Gama 1497

CAPE OF GOOD HOPE

Cabral 1500

ATLANTIC OCEAN

- Paris
- London
- Madrid
- Tangier
- Lisbon

Norsemen c. 1000

John Cabot 1497

ATLANTIC OCEAN

Columbus 1492

HUDSON'S BAY COMPANY

NEW FRANCE
- Quebec
- Boston
- BRITISH COLONIES
- Jamestown
- FLORIDA
- LOUISIANA

NEW SPAIN
- Mexico City
- CUBA
- ST. DOMINGUE
- JAMAICA

NEW Granada

NEW Castile

PERU
- Lima
- Santiago

GUIANA
- CAYENNE

BRAZIL
- Rio de Janeiro
- Buenos Aires

Rio de la Plata

Magellan 1520

PACIFIC OCEAN

©MAPS.com

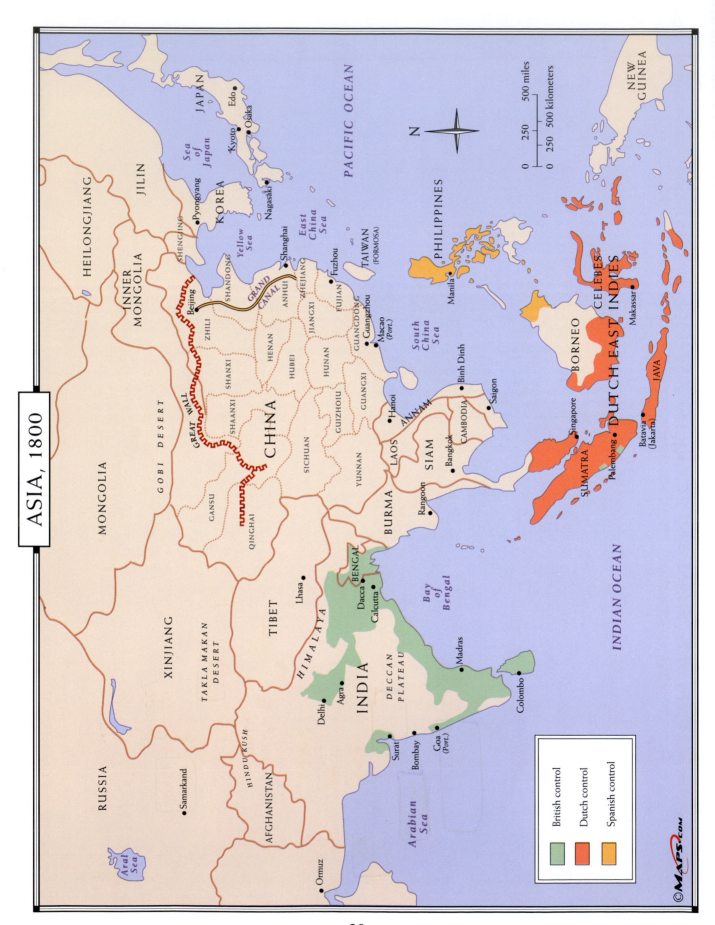

ASIA, 1800

PACIFIC OCEAN

RUSSIA

MONGOLIA

HEILONGJIANG

JILIN

INNER MONGOLIA

GOBI DESERT

JAPAN
- Edo
- Kyoto
- Osaka

Sea of Japan

KOREA
- Pyongyang
- Nagasaki

SHENGJING

Yellow Sea

ZHILI
- Beijing

SHANDONG

GRAND CANAL

SHANXI

SHAANXI

GANSU

QINGHAI

GREAT WALL

CHINA

HENAN

HUBEI

ANHUI
- Shanghai

East China Sea

ZHEJIANG

JIANGXI

FUJIAN
- Fuzhou

TAIWAN (FORMOSA)

SICHUAN

HUNAN

GUIZHOU

GUANGXI

GUANGDONG
- Guangzhou
- Macao (Port.)

YUNNAN

South China Sea

PHILIPPINES
- Manila

XINJIANG

TAKLA MAKAN DESERT

TIBET
- Lhasa

HIMALAYA

HINDU KUSH

AFGHANISTAN

- Samarkand

Aral Sea

- Ormuz

Arabian Sea

INDIA
- Delhi
- Agra
- Surat
- Bombay
- Goa (Port.)

DECCAN PLATEAU

- Madras

- Colombo

Bay of Bengal

BENGAL
- Dacca
- Calcutta

BURMA
- Rangoon

LAOS

SIAM
- Bangkok

ANNAM
- Hanoi
- Binh Dinh
- Saigon

CAMBODIA

SINGAPORE
- Singapore

SUMATRA
- Palembang

DUTCH EAST INDIES

BORNEO

CELEBES
- Makassar

JAVA
- Batavia (Jakarta)

NEW GUINEA

INDIAN OCEAN

N

| 0 | 250 | 500 miles |
| 0 | 250 | 500 kilometers |

Legend
- **British control**
- **Dutch control**
- **Spanish control**

©Maps.com

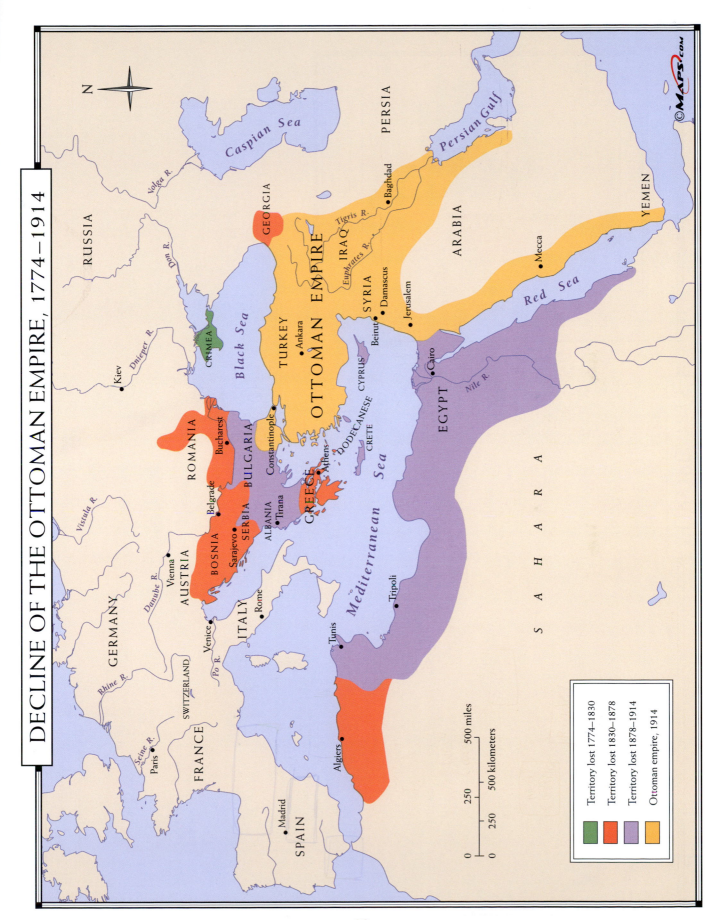

DECLINE OF THE OTTOMAN EMPIRE, 1774–1914

N

RUSSIA

Caspian Sea

Volga R.

Don R.

Dnieper R.

Kiev

Vistula R.

GERMANY

Rhine R.

Seine R.

Paris

FRANCE

SWITZERLAND

Po R.

Venice

ITALY

Rome

Danube R.

Vienna

AUSTRIA

BOSNIA

Sarajevo

SERBIA

Belgrade

ROMANIA

Bucharest

BULGARIA

ALBANIA

Tirana

GREECE

Athens

Constantinople

Black Sea

CRIMEA

TURKEY

Ankara

GEORGIA

OTTOMAN EMPIRE

IRAQ

Tigris R.

Euphrates R.

Baghdad

PERSIA

Persian Gulf

ARABIA

YEMEN

Mecca

Red Sea

SYRIA

Damascus

Beirut

Jerusalem

CYPRUS

Cairo

EGYPT

Nile R.

CRETE

DODECANESE

Mediterranean Sea

Tripoli

Tunis

Algiers

S A H A R A

SPAIN

Madrid

500 miles

500 kilometers

250

250

500

0

0

🟩	Territory lost 1774–1830
🟧	Territory lost 1830–1878
🟪	Territory lost 1878–1914
🟨	Ottoman empire, 1914

©MAPS.com

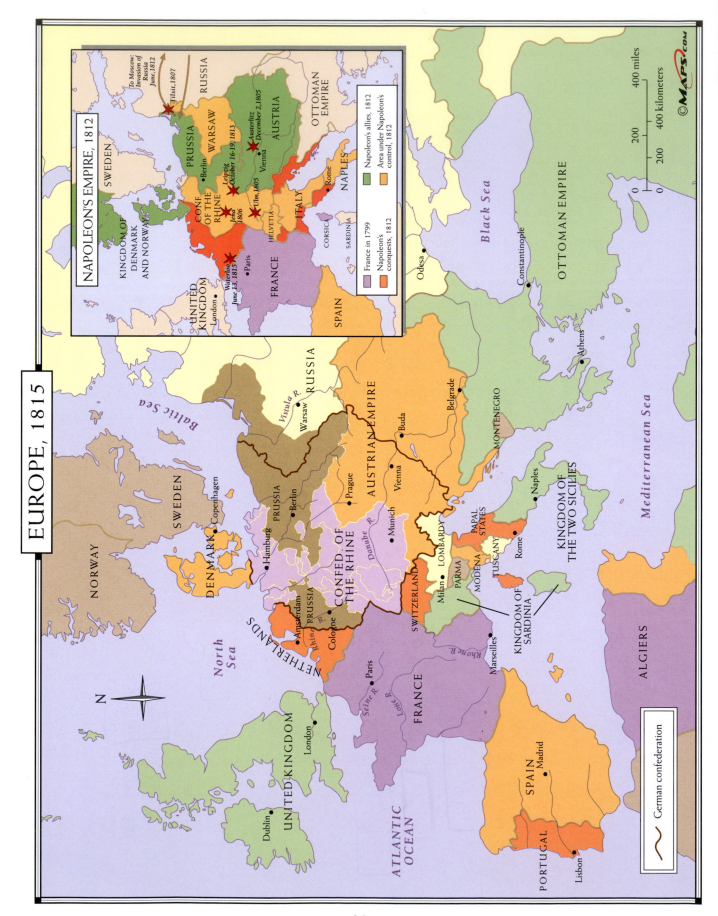

EUROPE, 1815

NAPOLEON'S EMPIRE, 1812

Legend:
- France in 1799
- Napoleon's conquests, 1812
- Napoleon's allies, 1812
- Area under Napoleon's control, 1812

To Moscow: Invasion of Russia June, 1812

Tilsit, 1807
Leipzig October 16-19, 1813
Austerlitz December 2, 1805
Ulm, 1805
Jena 1806
Waterloo June 13, 1815

SWEDEN
KINGDOM OF DENMARK AND NORWAY
RUSSIA
PRUSSIA
WARSAW
AUSTRIA
OTTOMAN EMPIRE
UNITED KINGDOM
CONF. OF THE RHINE
HELVETIA
ITALY
NAPLES
FRANCE
SPAIN
CORSICA
SARDINIA
London
Paris
Berlin
Vienna
Rome

400 miles
400 kilometers
200
200
0
0

©MAPS.com

German confederation

NORWAY
SWEDEN
DENMARK
UNITED KINGDOM
NETHERLANDS
PRUSSIA
CONFED. OF THE RHINE
PRUSSIA
SWITZERLAND
AUSTRIAN EMPIRE
RUSSIA
FRANCE
SPAIN
PORTUGAL
KINGDOM OF SARDINIA
LOMBARDY
PARMA
MODENA
TUSCANY
PAPAL STATES
KINGDOM OF THE TWO SICILIES
MONTENEGRO
OTTOMAN EMPIRE
ALGIERS

Dublin
London
Copenhagen
Hamburg
Amsterdam
Cologne
Berlin
Warsaw
Prague
Munich
Vienna
Buda
Belgrade
Milan
Rome
Naples
Marseilles
Paris
Madrid
Lisbon
Odesa
Constantinople
Athens

Atlantic Ocean
North Sea
Baltic Sea
Mediterranean Sea
Black Sea

Vistula R.
Danube R.
Rhine R.
Seine R.
Loire R.
Rhône R.

N

— 30 —

LATIN AMERICAN INDEPENDENCE, 19th CENTURY

UNITED STATES

Mississippi R.

Gulf of Mexico

MEXICO
(1821)

BRITISH
HONDURAS
(Br.)

Havana

CUBA
(1898)

HAITI
(1804)

DOMINICAN REP. (1844)

PUERTO RICO (Sp.)

ATLANTIC OCEAN

Vera
Cruz

Mexico City

JAMAICA
(Br.)

VIRGIN ISLANDS (Den. & Br.)

Belize

HONDURAS (1838)

GUATEMALA (1838)

Guatemala

Tegucigalpa

EL SALVADOR (1838)

NICARAGUA

Managua

San Jose

San Salvador

Caribbean Sea

CURACAO
(Dutch)

Caracas

TRINIDAD (Br.)

BRITISH GUIANA

DUTCH GUIANA

COSTA RICA (1838)

Panama

VENEZUELA
(1830)

Georgetown

Paramaribo

FRENCH GUIANA

Cayenne

Bogota

COLOMBIA
(1819)

Quito

ECUADOR
(1822)

Amazon R.

A N D E S

PERU
(1821)

Lima

La Paz

BOLIVIA
(1825)

Lake Titicaca

A N D E S

BRAZIL
(Monarchy 1822–1889;
Republic 1889)

Recife

Bahia

Paraguay R.

PARAGUAY
(1811)

Rio de Janeiro

Asunción

PACIFIC OCEAN

CHILE
(1818)

Parana R.

Santiago

Buenos Aires

URUGUAY
(1828)

Montevideo

ARGENTINA
(1810)

ATLANTIC OCEAN

N

0   500   1,000 miles

0   500   1,000 kilometers

FALKLAND IS. (Br.)

©Maps.com

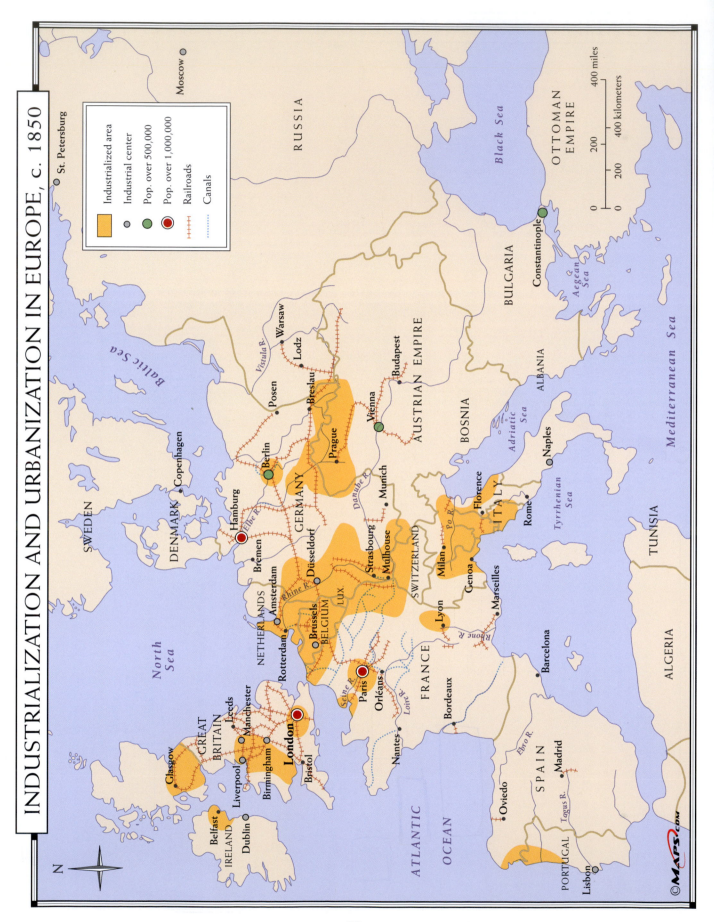

INDUSTRIALIZATION AND URBANIZATION IN EUROPE, c. 1850

Legend:
- Industrialized area
- Industrial center
- Pop. over 500,000
- Pop. over 1,000,000
- Railroads
- Canals

St. Petersburg

Moscow

RUSSIA

SWEDEN

Baltic Sea

Warsaw

Vistula R.

Lodz

Posen

Breslau

DENMARK

Copenhagen

Berlin

GERMANY

Prague

Vienna

AUSTRIAN EMPIRE

Budapest

BULGARIA

Black Sea

OTTOMAN EMPIRE

Constantinople

Aegean Sea

ALBANIA

BOSNIA

Hamburg

Bremen

Elbe R.

Düsseldorf

Rhine R.

Amsterdam

NETHERLANDS

Rotterdam

LUX.

BELGIUM

Brussels

Munich

Danube R.

Strasbourg

Mulhouse

SWITZERLAND

Milan

Po R.

Genoa

Florence

ITALY

Rome

Naples

Tyrrhenian Sea

Adriatic Sea

Mediterranean Sea

TUNISIA

ALGERIA

Lyon

Rhone R.

Marseilles

FRANCE

Seine R.

Paris

Orléans

Loire R.

Nantes

Bordeaux

Barcelona

Ebro R.

Madrid

SPAIN

Oviedo

Tagus R.

PORTUGAL

Lisbon

ATLANTIC OCEAN

North Sea

GREAT BRITAIN

Glasgow

Leeds

Manchester

Liverpool

Birmingham

London

Bristol

IRELAND

Belfast

Dublin

400 miles

400 kilometers

200

200

0

0

N

©MAPS.com

– 32 –

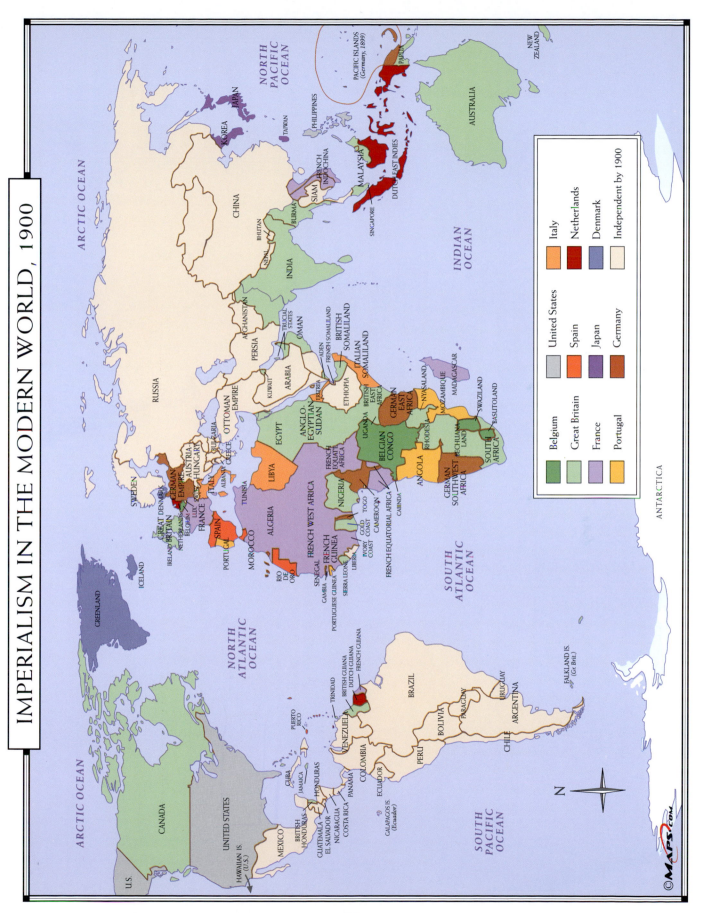

IMPERIALISM IN THE MODERN WORLD, 1900

Legend

Belgium	United States	Italy	
Great Britain	Spain	Netherlands	
France	Japan	Denmark	
Portugal	Germany	Independent by 1900	

ARCTIC OCEAN

NORTH PACIFIC OCEAN

PACIFIC ISLANDS (Germany, 1899)

PAPUA

NEW ZEALAND

AUSTRALIA

JAPAN

KOREA

TAIWAN

PHILIPPINES

CHINA

SIAM

FRENCH INDOCHINA

BURMA

BHUTAN

NEPAL

INDIA

MALAYSIA

DUTCH EAST INDIES

SINGAPORE

AFGHANISTAN

PERSIA

OTTOMAN EMPIRE

INDIAN OCEAN

RUSSIA

SWEDEN

GREAT DENMARK

GERMAN EMPIRE

AUSTRIA-HUNGARY

ITALY

ALBANIA

GREECE

BULGARIA

GREAT BRITAIN

IRELAND

NETHERLANDS

BELGIUM

LUX.

FRANCE

SPAIN

PORTUGAL

MOROCCO

TUNISIA

ALGERIA

LIBYA

RIO DE ORO

SENEGAL

GAMBIA

PORTUGUESE GUINEA

FRENCH GUINEA

SIERRA LEONE

LIBERIA

IVORY COAST

GOLD COAST

TOGO

CAMEROON

NIGERIA

FRENCH WEST AFRICA

FRENCH EQUATORIAL AFRICA

CABINDA

ANGOLA

GERMAN SOUTHWEST AFRICA

BECHUANA-LAND

RHODESIA

SOUTH AFRICA

BASUTOLAND

SWAZILAND

GERMAN EAST AFRICA

BELGIAN CONGO

UGANDA

BRITISH EAST AFRICA

NYASALAND

MOZAMBIQUE

MADAGASCAR

ANGLO-EGYPTIAN SUDAN

EGYPT

ETHIOPIA

ERITREA

ITALIAN SOMALILAND

BRITISH SOMALILAND

FRENCH SOMALILAND

ADEN

OMAN

TRUCIAL STATES

ARABIA

KUWAIT

ICELAND

GREENLAND

NORTH ATLANTIC OCEAN

SOUTH ATLANTIC OCEAN

CANADA

UNITED STATES

U.S.

HAWAIIAN IS. (U.S.)

MEXICO

BRITISH HONDURAS

GUATEMALA

EL SALVADOR

NICARAGUA

COSTA RICA

HONDURAS

PANAMA

JAMAICA

CUBA

PUERTO RICO

TRINIDAD

VENEZUELA

COLOMBIA

ECUADOR

GALAPAGOS IS. (Ecuador)

PERU

BRAZIL

BOLIVIA

PARAGUAY

BRITISH GUIANA

DUTCH GUIANA

FRENCH GUIANA

URUGUAY

ARGENTINA

CHILE

FALKLAND IS. (Gr. Brit.)

SOUTH PACIFIC OCEAN

ANTARCTICA

N

©Maps.com

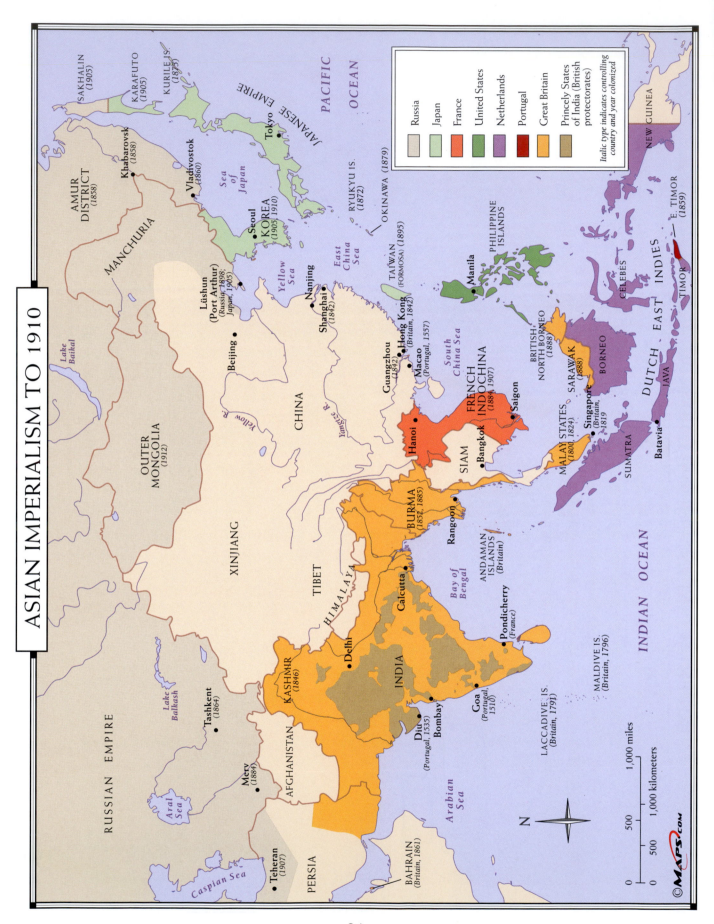

ASIAN IMPERIALISM TO 1910

Legend:
- Russia
- Japan
- France
- United States
- Netherlands
- Portugal
- Great Britain
- Princely States of India (British protectorates)

Italic type indicates controlling country and year colonized

PACIFIC OCEAN

JAPANESE EMPIRE

SAKHALIN (1905)
KARAFUTO (1905)
KURILE IS. (1875)

AMUR DISTRICT (1858)

MANCHURIA

Khabarovsk (1858)
Vladivostok (1860)

Sea of Japan

Tokyo

Seoul
KOREA (1905 1910)

RYUKYU IS. (1872)
OKINAWA (1879)

Lake Baikal

Lüshun (Port Arthur) (Russia, 1898; Japan, 1905)

Yellow Sea

Nanjing

Shanghai (1842)

East China Sea

TAIWAN (FORMOSA) (1895)

PHILIPPINE ISLANDS

Manila

Beijing

CHINA

Guangzhou (1842)
Hong Kong (Britain, 1842)
Macao (Portugal, 1557)

South China Sea

FRENCH INDOCHINA (1884, 1907)

Hanoi

Saigon

BRITISH NORTH BORNEO (1888)

SARAWAK (1888)

BORNEO

NEW GUINEA

E. TIMOR (1859)
TIMOR

CELEBES

DUTCH EAST INDIES

OUTER MONGOLIA (1912)

XINJIANG

TIBET

HIMALAYA

BURMA (1852, 1885)

Rangoon

SIAM

Bangkok

MALAY STATES (1800, 1824)

Singapore (Britain, 1819)

SUMATRA

JAVA

Batavia

RUSSIAN EMPIRE

Lake Balkash

Tashkent (1864)

KASHMIR (1846)

Delhi

INDIA

Calcutta

ANDAMAN ISLANDS (Britain)

Bay of Bengal

Pondicherry (France)

INDIAN OCEAN

Yellow R.

Yangtze R.

AFGHANISTAN

Aral Sea

Merv (1884)

Bombay

Goa (Portugal, 1510)

Diu (Portugal, 1535)

MALDIVE IS. (Britain, 1796)

LACCADIVE IS. (Britain, 1791)

BAHRAIN (Britain, 1861)

Arabian Sea

Teheran (1907)

PERSIA

Caspian Sea

1,000 miles
1,000 kilometers

500

500

0

0

N

©MAPS.com

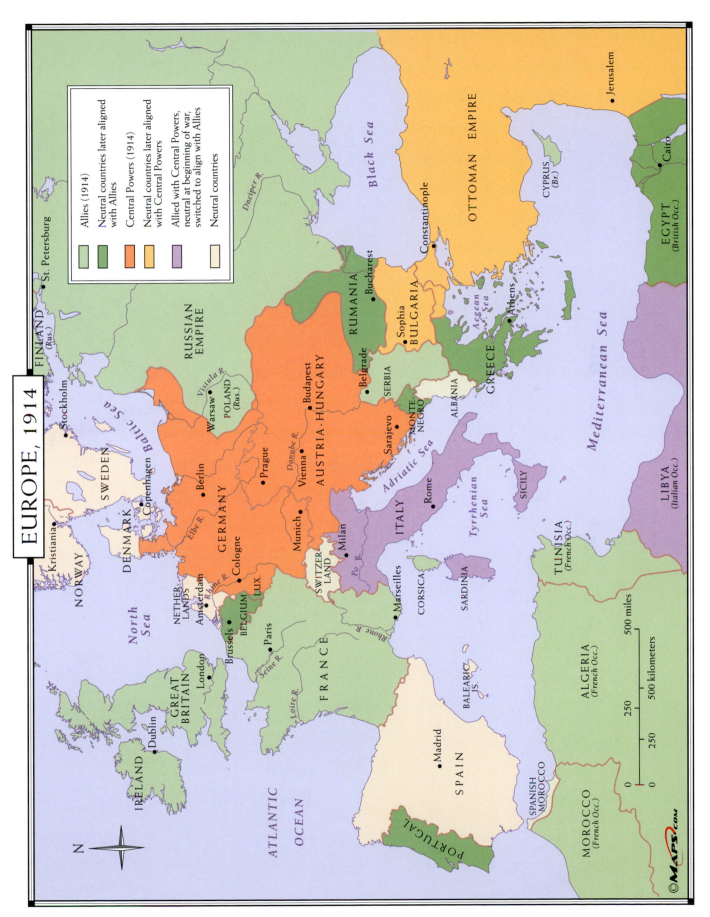

EUROPE, 1914

Legend:
- Allies (1914)
- Neutral countries later aligned with Allies
- Central Powers (1914)
- Neutral countries later aligned with Central Powers
- Allied with Central Powers, neutral at beginning of war, switched to align with Allies
- Neutral countries

Labels on map:

FINLAND (Rus.) • St. Petersburg

RUSSIAN EMPIRE

Dnieper R.

Black Sea

OTTOMAN EMPIRE

• Jerusalem

CYPRUS (Br.)

• Cairo

EGYPT (British Occ.)

Constantinople •

RUMANIA • Bucharest

Sophia • BULGARIA

Aegean Sea

Athens •

GREECE

Mediterranean Sea

LIBYA (Italian Occ.)

Vistula R.

Warsaw •

POLAND (Rus.)

Belgrade •

SERBIA

Sarajevo •

MONTE-NEGRO

ALBANIA

Adriatic Sea

Stockholm •

Baltic Sea

SWEDEN

Budapest •

Danube R.

Vienna •

AUSTRIA-HUNGARY

Kristiania •

NORWAY

DENMARK

Copenhagen •

Elbe R.

Berlin •

Prague •

GERMANY

Munich •

Milan •

ITALY

Rome •

Tyrrhenian Sea

SICILY

TUNISIA (French Occ.)

North Sea

NETHER-LANDS

Amsterdam •

Cologne

Rhine R.

LUX.

BELGIUM

Brussels •

SWITZER-LAND

Po R.

CORSICA

SARDINIA

ALGERIA (French Occ.)

London •

GREAT BRITAIN

Paris •

Seine R.

FRANCE

Marseilles •

Rhône R.

BALEARIC IS.

IRELAND

Dublin •

Loire R.

Madrid •

SPAIN

SPANISH MOROCCO

MOROCCO (French Occ.)

PORTUGAL

ATLANTIC OCEAN

N

500 miles
500 kilometers
250
250
0
0

©MAPS.com

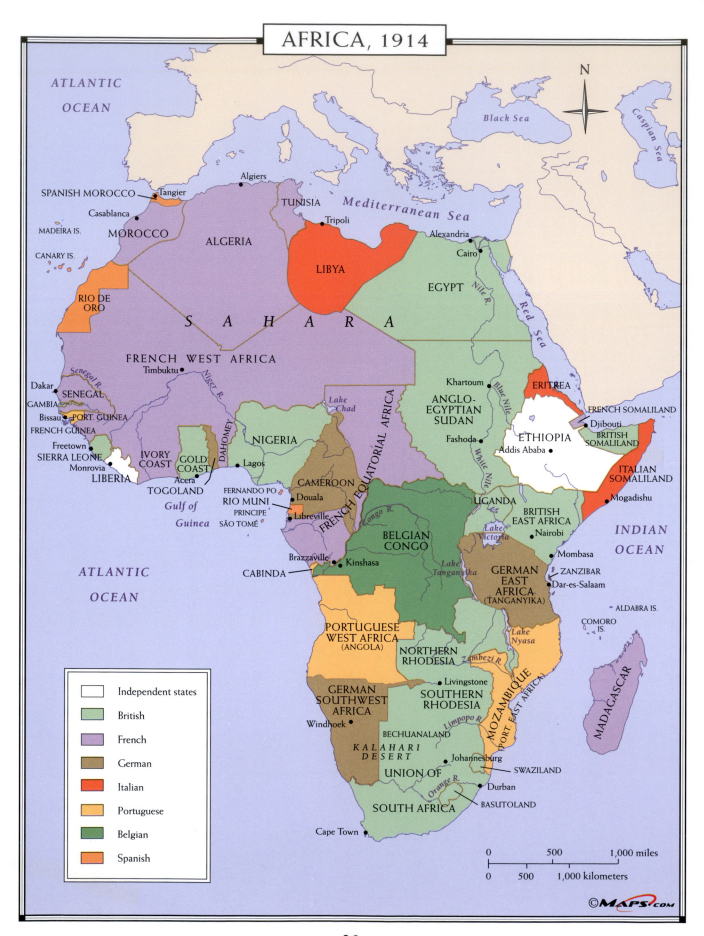

AFRICA, 1914

Legend (Independent states and colonial powers):
- Independent states
- British
- French
- German
- Italian
- Portuguese
- Belgian
- Spanish

ATLANTIC OCEAN

Mediterranean Sea

Black Sea

Caspian Sea

SPANISH MOROCCO
Tangier
Algiers
TUNISIA
Casablanca
MOROCCO
ALGERIA
LIBYA
Tripoli
Alexandria
Cairo
EGYPT
MADEIRA IS.
CANARY IS.
RIO DE ORO
S A H A R A
FRENCH WEST AFRICA
Timbuktu
Nile R.
Red Sea
Dakar
SENEGAL
Senegal R.
Niger R.
Khartoum
Blue Nile
ERITREA
FRENCH SOMALILAND
GAMBIA
Bissau
PORT. GUINEA
FRENCH GUINEA
Lake Chad
NIGERIA
ANGLO-EGYPTIAN SUDAN
Djibouti
BRITISH SOMALILAND
Freetown
SIERRA LEONE
Monrovia
LIBERIA
IVORY COAST
GOLD COAST
Accra
DAHOMEY
Lagos
CAMEROON
FRENCH EQUATORIAL AFRICA
Fashoda
White Nile
ETHIOPIA
Addis Ababa
ITALIAN SOMALILAND
Mogadishu
TOGOLAND
Gulf of Guinea
FERNANDO PO
RIO MUNI
Douala
PRINCIPE
SÃO TOMÉ
Libreville
Congo R.
UGANDA
BRITISH EAST AFRICA
Nairobi
INDIAN OCEAN
Lake Victoria
BELGIAN CONGO
Mombasa
Brazzaville
Kinshasa
CABINDA
Lake Tanganyika
GERMAN EAST AFRICA (TANGANYIKA)
ZANZIBAR
Dar-es-Salaam
ATLANTIC OCEAN
ALDABRA IS.
COMORO IS.
PORTUGUESE WEST AFRICA (ANGOLA)
Lake Nyasa
NORTHERN RHODESIA
Zambezi R.
Livingstone
MOZAMBIQUE (PORT. EAST AFRICA)
MADAGASCAR
GERMAN SOUTHWEST AFRICA
SOUTHERN RHODESIA
Windhoek
BECHUANALAND
KALAHARI DESERT
Limpopo R.
SWAZILAND
Johannesburg
UNION OF
Orange R.
Durban
BASUTOLAND
SOUTH AFRICA
Cape Town

N

0   500   1,000 miles
0   500   1,000 kilometers

©Maps.com

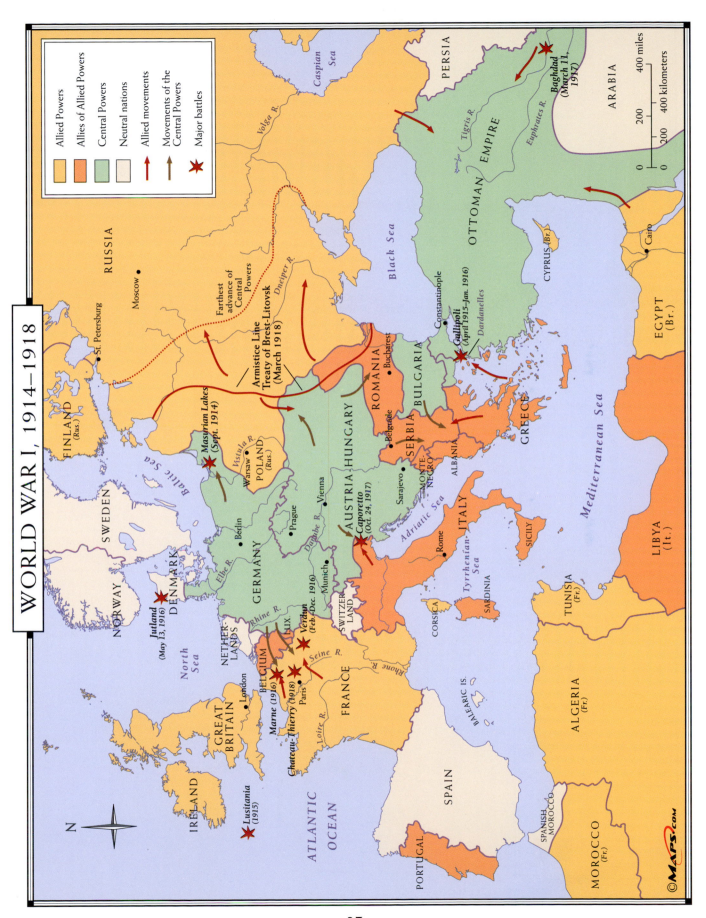

WORLD WAR I, 1914–1918

Legend:
- Allied Powers
- Allies of Allied Powers
- Central Powers
- Neutral nations
- Allied movements
- Movements of the Central Powers
- Major battles

Labels on map:

RUSSIA
Moscow
St. Petersburg
FINLAND (Rus.)
NORWAY
SWEDEN
Baltic Sea
DENMARK
Jutland (May 13, 1916)
North Sea
NETHER-LANDS
GREAT BRITAIN
London
IRELAND
ATLANTIC OCEAN
Lusitania (1915)
BELGIUM
LUX.
FRANCE
Paris
Marne (1916)
Château-Thierry (1918)
Verdun (Feb.–Dec. 1916)
Seine R.
Loire R.
Rhône R.
Rhine R.
Elbe R.
GERMANY
Berlin
Prague
Munich
SWITZER-LAND
Vienna
Danube R.
Warsaw
POLAND (Rus.)
Vistula R.
Masurian Lakes (Sept. 1914)
Dnieper R.
Volga R.
Caspian Sea
Farthest advance of Central Powers
Armistice Line Treaty of Brest-Litovsk (March 1918)
AUSTRIA-HUNGARY
Caporetto (Oct. 24, 1917)
ITALY
Rome
Adriatic Sea
Tyrrhenian Sea
SARDINIA
CORSICA
BALEARIC IS.
SICILY
Mediterranean Sea
ROMANIA
Bucharest
Belgrade
SERBIA
Sarajevo
MONTE-NEGRO
ALBANIA
BULGARIA
GREECE
Black Sea
Constantinople
Dardanelles
Gallipoli (April 1915–Jan. 1916)
OTTOMAN EMPIRE
PERSIA
Tigris R.
Euphrates R.
Baghdad (March 11, 1917)
ARABIA
CYPRUS (Br.)
Cairo
EGYPT (Br.)
LIBYA (It.)
TUNISIA (Fr.)
ALGERIA (Fr.)
MOROCCO (Fr.)
SPANISH MOROCCO
SPAIN
PORTUGAL

Scale: 400 miles / 400 kilometers
N

©MAPS.com

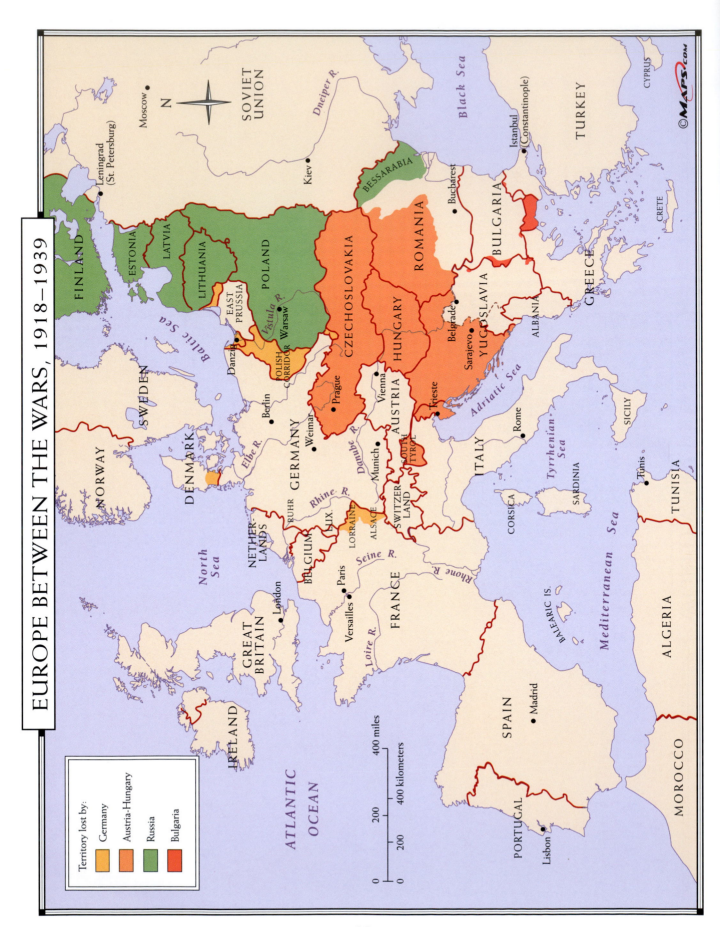

EUROPE BETWEEN THE WARS, 1918–1939

SOVIET UNION

Moscow

Leningrad (St. Petersburg)

Kiev

Dneiper R.

FINLAND

ESTONIA

LATVIA

LITHUANIA

Baltic Sea

NORWAY

SWEDEN

DENMARK

EAST PRUSSIA

Danzig

POLISH CORRIDOR

Vistula R.

Warsaw

POLAND

Berlin

GERMANY

Weimar

Elbe R.

Rhine R.

RUHR

LUX.

Danube R.

Munich

Prague

Vienna

CZECHOSLOVAKIA

HUNGARY

AUSTRIA

SWITZER-LAND

SOUTH TYROL

ALSACE

LORRAINE

BELGIUM

NETHER-LANDS

Seine R.

Paris

Versailles

Loire R.

Rhone R.

FRANCE

GREAT BRITAIN

London

IRELAND

North Sea

ATLANTIC OCEAN

BESSARABIA

ROMANIA

Bucharest

BULGARIA

Belgrade

Sarajevo

YUGOSLAVIA

Trieste

Adriatic Sea

ALBANIA

GREECE

Black Sea

Istanbul (Constantinople)

TURKEY

CYPRUS

CRETE

ITALY

Rome

CORSICA

SARDINIA

Tyrrhenian Sea

SICILY

Mediterranean Sea

Tunis

TUNISIA

ALGERIA

MOROCCO

SPAIN

Madrid

PORTUGAL

Lisbon

BALEARIC IS.

Territory lost by:
- Germany
- Austria-Hungary
- Russia
- Bulgaria

400 miles

400 kilometers

200

200

0

0

©MAPS.com

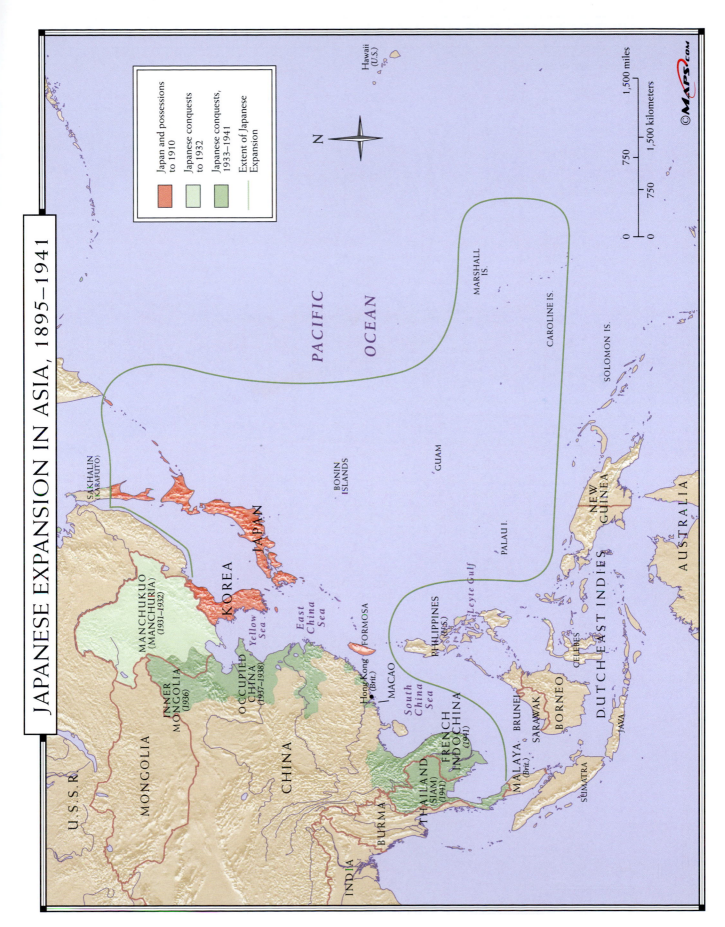

JAPANESE EXPANSION IN ASIA, 1895–1941

Legend:
- Japan and possessions to 1910
- Japanese conquests to 1932
- Japanese conquests, 1933–1941
- Extent of Japanese Expansion

1,500 miles

1,500 kilometers

750

750

0

0

©MAPS.com

Hawaii (U.S.)

N

PACIFIC OCEAN

MARSHALL IS.

CAROLINE IS.

SOLOMON IS.

GUAM

BONIN ISLANDS

PALAU I.

NEW GUINEA

AUSTRALIA

SAKHALIN (KARAFUTO)

MANCHUKUO (MANCHURIA) (1931–1932)

INNER MONGOLIA (1936)

KOREA

JAPAN

OCCUPIED CHINA (1937–1938)

Yellow Sea

East China Sea

FORMOSA

Hong Kong (Brit.)

MACAO

South China Sea

PHILIPPINES (U.S.)

Leyte Gulf

MONGOLIA

U.S.S.R.

CHINA

INDIA

BURMA

THAILAND (SIAM) (1941)

FRENCH INDOCHINA (1941)

MALAYA (Brit.)

BRUNEI

SARAWAK

BORNEO

CELEBES

DUTCH EAST INDIES

SUMATRA

JAVA

WORLD WAR II, EUROPEAN THEATER, 1940–1945

Legend:
- Axis nations
- Occupied by Axis
- Allied nations
- Neutral nations
- Allied forces
- Axis forces
- ★ Major battles

N

Leningrad (Sept. 1941–Jan. 1944)

FINLAND

SWEDEN

NORWAY

DENMARK

ESTONIA

LATVIA

LITHUANIA

SOVIET UNION

EAST PRUSSIA

Danzig

POLAND

Warsaw

Kiev

to Stalingrad (Aug. 1942–Jan. 1943)

IRELAND

GREAT BRITAIN

Battle of Britain (Aug.–Oct. 1940)

London

Amsterdam

NETHERLANDS

BELGIUM

GERMANY

Berlin

Prague

BOHEMIA MORAVIA

SLOVAKIA

Munich

Vienna

HUNGARY

ROMANIA

Bucharest

North Sea

Baltic Sea

ATLANTIC OCEAN

Cherbourg

D-Day (June 1944)

Battle of the Bulge (Dec. 1944)

LUX.

Paris

FRANCE

Vichy

SWITZ.

ITALY

YUGOSLAVIA

Belgrade

BULGARIA

Black Sea

Istanbul

PORTUGAL

SPAIN

Madrid

CORSICA

Rome

SARDINIA

ALBANIA

GREECE

Athens

TURKEY

Mediterranean Sea

SICILY

SPANISH MOROCCO

Oran

MOROCCO

ALGERIA

TUNISIA

Tripoli

LIBYA

El Alamein (Oct.–Nov. 1942)

EGYPT

0   200   400 miles

0   200   400 kilometers

©Maps.com

– 40 –

WORLD WAR II IN THE PACIFIC, 1941–1945

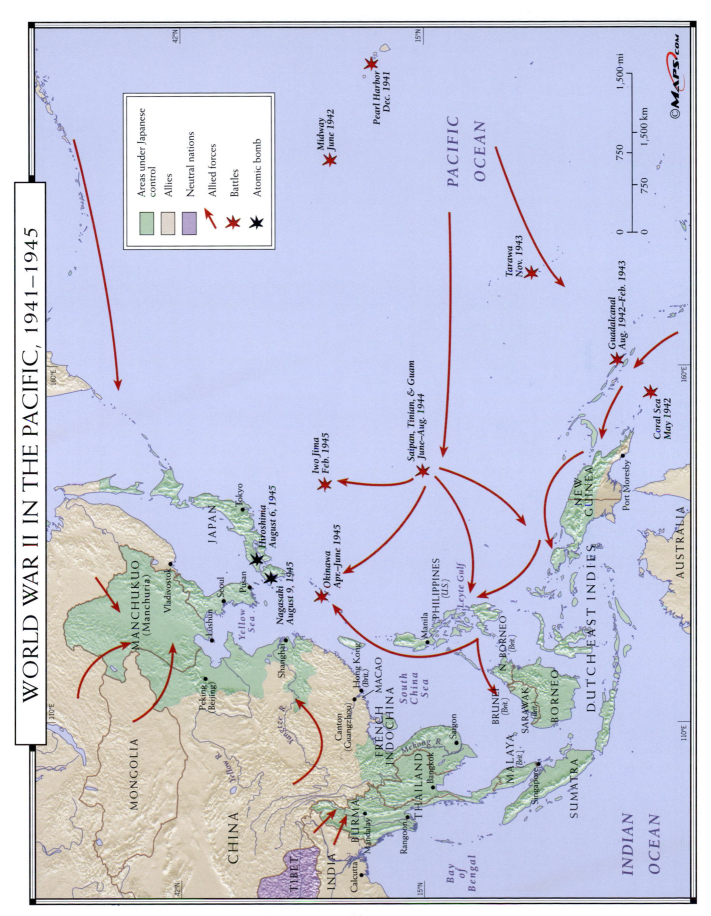

Legend:
- Areas under Japanese control
- Allies
- Neutral nations
- Allied forces
- Battles
- Atomic bomb

Labels on map:

PACIFIC OCEAN

Pearl Harbor Dec. 1941

Midway June 1942

Tarawa Nov. 1943

Guadalcanal Aug. 1942–Feb. 1943

Coral Sea May 1942

Saipan, Tinian, & Guam June–Aug. 1944

Iwo Jima Feb. 1945

Hiroshima August 6, 1945

Nagasaki August 9, 1945

Okinawa Apr.–June 1945

Leyte Gulf

NEW GUINEA

Port Moresby

AUSTRALIA

PHILIPPINES (U.S.)

Manila

DUTCH EAST INDIES

N. BORNEO (Brit.)

BORNEO

SARAWAK (Brit.)

BRUNEI (Brit.)

MALAYA (Brit.)

Singapore

SUMATRA

THAILAND

Bangkok

FRENCH INDO-CHINA

Saigon

Mekong R.

South China Sea

MACAO

Hong Kong (Brit.)

Canton (Guangzhou)

Yangtze R.

Shanghai

CHINA

Peking (Beijing)

Yellow R.

MONGOLIA

TIBET

INDIA

Calcutta

Rangoon

BURMA

Mandalay

Bay of Bengal

INDIAN OCEAN

MANCHUKUO (Manchuria)

Lüshun

Vladivostok

Seoul

Pusan

Yellow Sea

JAPAN

Tokyo

Scale:
1,500 mi
1,500 km
750
750
0

©MAPS.com

INDEPENDENT STATES TO 1991

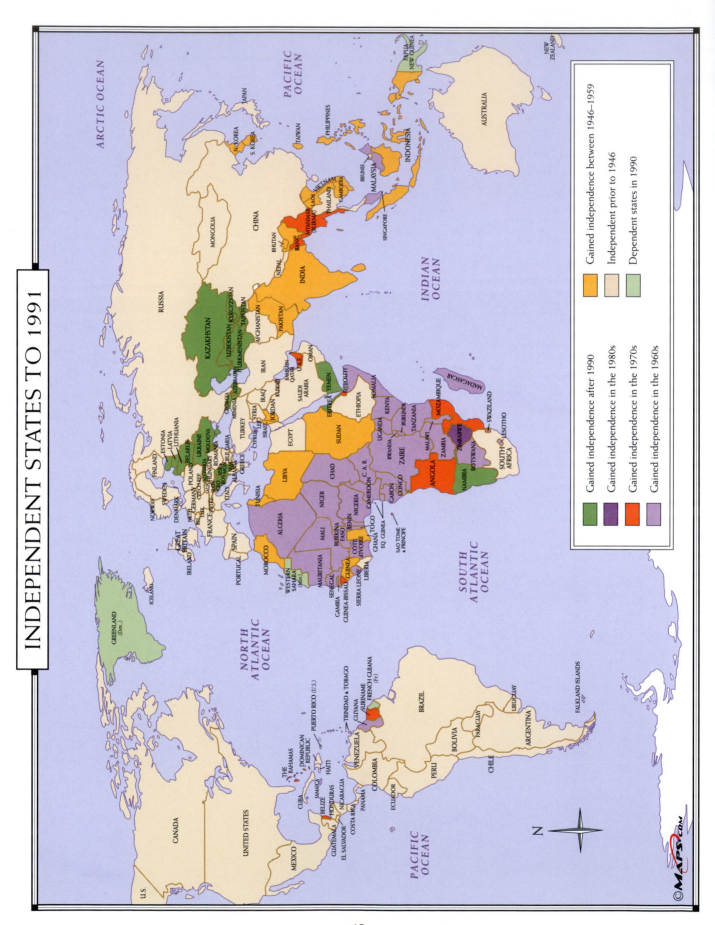

Legend:

Gained independence between 1946–1959 — orange

Independent prior to 1946 — tan

Dependent states in 1990 — green

Gained independence after 1990 — green

Gained independence in the 1980s — purple

Gained independence in the 1970s — red/orange

Gained independence in the 1960s — light purple

COLD WAR EUROPE, 1946–1990

N

Legend:
- NATO Alliance
- Warsaw Pact Nations

ICELAND

NORWAY
Oslo

SWEDEN
Stockholm

FINLAND
Helsinki

Leningrad

North Sea

DENMARK
Copenhagen

Riga

Vilnius

Minsk

SOVIET UNION

IRELAND
Dublin

UNITED KINGDOM
London

NETHERLANDS
Amsterdam

Elbe R.

Berlin
EAST GERMANY

Vistula R.
Warsaw
POLAND

Kiev

ATLANTIC OCEAN

BELGIUM
Brussels
LUX.
Bonn
WEST GERMANY

Rhin R.

Prague
CZECHOSLOVAKIA

Paris
Seine R.

Loire R.

Munich

Danube R.
Vienna
AUSTRIA

Bratislava
Budapest
HUNGARY

Kishinev

FRANCE

SWITZ.
Geneva

ROMANIA

Po R.

Belgrade
YUGOSLAVIA
Sarajevo

Bucharest

BULGARIA
Sofia

PORTUGAL

SPAIN
(Joined NATO in 1982)
Madrid

Tiber R.
Rome
ITALY

Skopje

Istanbul

Lisbon

Tirana
ALBANIA
(Withdrew from
Warsaw Pact in 1968)

TURKEY

GREECE

Mediterranean Sea

Athens

ALGERIA

0   200   400 miles

0   200   400 kilometers

©MAPS.com

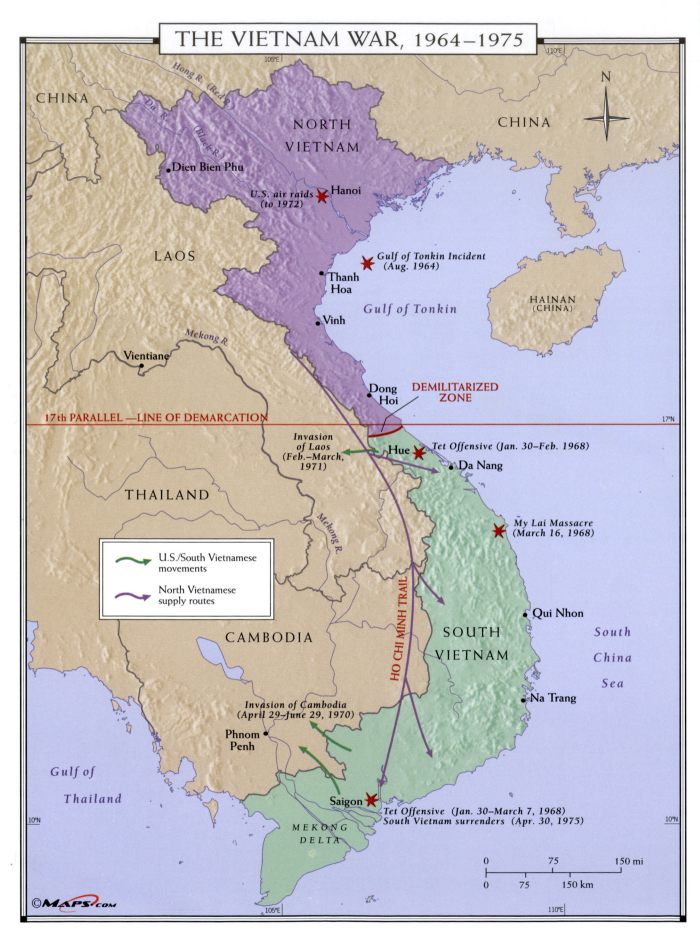

THE VIETNAM WAR, 1964–1975

CHINA

Hong R. (Red R.)

CHINA

N

Da R.

(Black R.)

NORTH
VIETNAM

• Dien Bien Phu

U.S. air raids
(to 1972) ★ Hanoi

LAOS

★ Gulf of Tonkin Incident
(Aug. 1964)

• Thanh
Hoa

Gulf of Tonkin

HAINAN
(CHINA)

• Vinh

Mekong R.

Vientiane •

• Dong
Hoi

**DEMILITARIZED
ZONE**

17th PARALLEL —LINE OF DEMARCATION 17°N

*Invasion
of Laos
(Feb.–March,
1971)*

★ Hue ★ *Tet Offensive (Jan. 30–Feb. 1968)*

• Da Nang

THAILAND

*My Lai Massacre
(March 16, 1968)* ★

Mekong R.

U.S./South Vietnamese
movements

North Vietnamese
supply routes

HO CHI MINH TRAIL

• Qui Nhon

CAMBODIA

SOUTH
VIETNAM

South
China
Sea

• Na Trang

*Invasion of Cambodia
(April 29–June 29, 1970)*

Phnom
Penh •

Gulf
of
Thailand

Saigon • ★

*MEKONG
DELTA*

*Tet Offensive (Jan. 30–March 7, 1968)
South Vietnam surrenders (Apr. 30, 1975)*

10°N 10°N

0   75   150 mi

0   75   150 km

©Maps.com

105°E   110°E

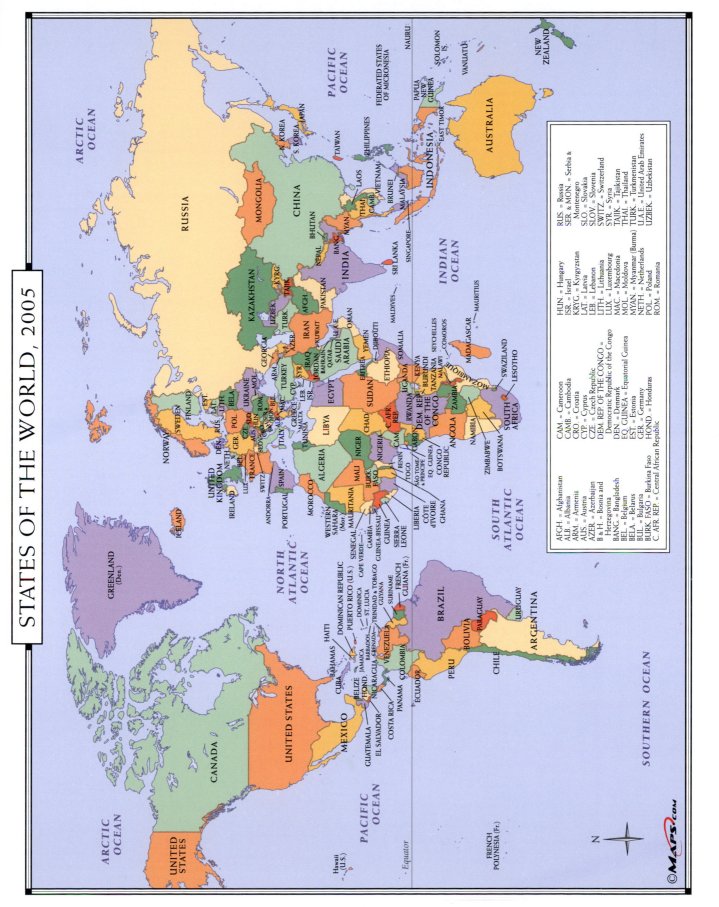

STATES OF THE WORLD, 2005